A Gift For:

Phil

From:

1/21/2009
63 yrs. old

PERFECT PAIRS
a photographic celebration

BOK6005

Love is blind,
but marriage restores its sight.

Geog Christoph Lichenberg

 THE PHILADELPHIA STORY [1940]
Cary Grant & Katharine Hepburn

FILM FACT: The Philadelphia Story was Katharine Hepburn's big comback film after she had been labeled "box office poison" in the late 1930s. With her unerring instinct for quality, Katharine purchased the rights to the Philip Barry play as a vehicle for herself, and effectively controlled this wonderful MGM movie.

> Passion is the element in which we live;
> without it, we hardly vegetate.
>
> *Lord Byron*

 ## Cover Girl [1944]
Gene Kelly & Rita Hayworth

FILM FACT: On loan from MGM, Gene Kelly got free reign from Columbia Pictures for this movie. Ever inventive, he had several of the soundstage walls removed so that he, Rita Hayworth, and Phil Silvers could dance along an entire street in one take. And Kelly used trick photography so he could dance with himself in the famous "alter-ego" scene.

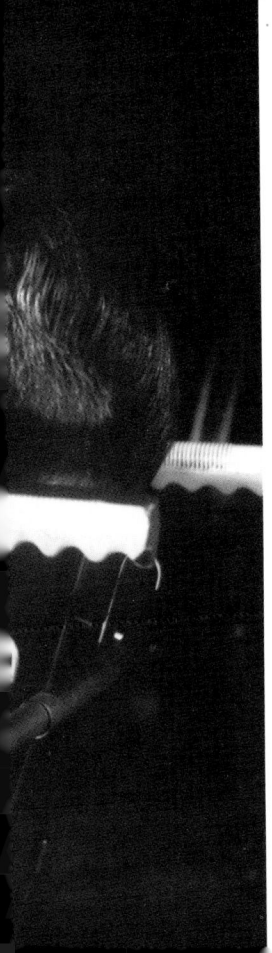

STELLA: When two people love each other, they come together—WHAM—like two taxis on Broadway.

 REAR WINDOW [1954]
James Stewart & Grace Kelly

FILM FACT: A cinema masterpiece that began when director Alfred Hitchcock explored the possibility of making a movie on one set from a fixed vantage point, pairing James Stewart with Grace Kelly.

> What will not woman,
> gentle woman dare;
> when strong affection
> stirs her spirit up?
>
> *Robert Southey*

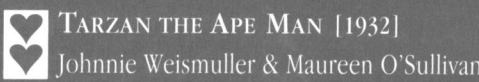

TARZAN THE APE MAN [1932]
Johnnie Weismuller & Maureen O'Sullivan

FILM FACT: Five-time Olympic gold-medal swimmer Johnnie Weismuller was the sixth actor to portray Tarzan. He played the part nineteen times, six of them paired with Maureen O'Sullivan as Jane.

ALICIA: Say it again, it keeps me awake.
DEVLIN: I love you.

 NOTORIOUS [1946]
Cary Grant & Ingrid Bergman

FILM FACT: Genius director Alfred Hitchcock managed to extend the infamous three-second screen kiss rule right under the noses of the censors with one of the longest kisses ever filmed. He achieved it by having Grant and Bergman kiss, talk, kiss, walk, kiss, nibble, kiss and so forth, and at no point did it last more than three seconds, so the now famous love scene got through untouched.

GIRL: What are you rebelling against, Johnny?
JOHNNY: Whaddya got?

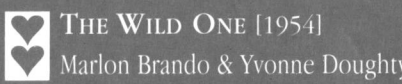
THE WILD ONE [1954]
Marlon Brando & Yvonne Doughty

FILM FACT: Based on a true incident in 1947, when over 3,000 motorcyclists opted to celebrate the 4th of July by riding into a small California township.

PRUDENCE WORTH: …you thought that living with me would be tiresome and dull after a while, tiresome and dull because all I knew, raised since a baby here on the farm, was our belief that people love, marry, and stay together forever after that…

QUIRT EVANS: Are you ever going to run down and let me talk!

 ANGEL AND THE BADMAN [1947]
John Wayne & Gail Russell

FILM FACT: The first movie that John Wayne produced also produced the rumor that The Duke was romantically linked with co-star Gail Russell.

MARGUERITE: It's you. It's not a dream.

ARMAND: No, it's not a dream. I'm here with you in my arms, at last.

MARGUERITE: At last.

ARMAND: You're weak.

MARGUERITE: No, no. Strong. (She collapses into a chair.) It's my heart. It's not used to being happy.

CAMILLE [1937]
Robert Taylor & Greta Garbo

FILM FACT: While *Camille* was one of Garbo's greatest commercial and critical successes, she was to go on and make only three more films before retiring from the screen in 1941.

Speak low if you speak love.

Don Pedro

Beau Ideal [1931]
Ralph Forbes & Loretta Young

Film Fact: Despite the alluring gaze of the young Ms. Young, the film is thought to have lost nearly $350,000. As a result, the Geste family didn't return to the big screen until 1939 for a remake of Beau Geste.

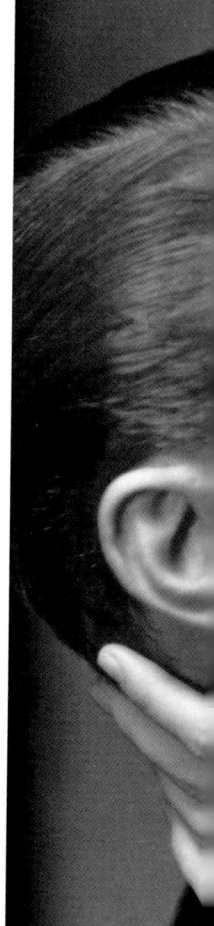

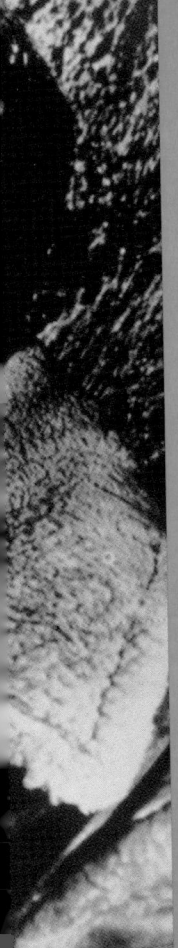

When two people love each other,
they don't look at each other,
they look in the same direction.

Ginger Rogers

 FOR WHOM THE BELL TOLLS [1943]
Gary Cooper & Ingrid Bergman

FILM FACT: In the closing scene, Cooper rides his horse through enemy gunfire, the horse falls and breaks its leg. The only horse they could get to do the stunt was brown, and Cooper's horse throughout the film was a dapple-gray—so they painted it!

> What do women want?
>
> *Sigmund Freud*

 **MADAME BOVARY** [1949]
Louis Jourdan & Jennifer Jones

FILM FACT: MGM managed to get around the censorship issues that would have prevented any adaptation of Flaubert's *Madame Bovary* by the clever addition of a prologue and epilogue, which served to illustrate the story as being a work of fiction.

> Love knows not its
> own depth until the
> hour of separation.
>
> *Kahlil Gibran*

 ## WEST SIDE STORY [1960]
Richard Beymer & Natalie Wood

FILM FACT: Natalie Wood was instantly loved as Maria, while Richard Beymer found himself heavily criticized at the time as the tragic Tony—who provides us today with a classic glimpse of 1950s yearning.

JUDY: Nothing can hurt us now. What we have can't be destroyed. That's our victory—our victory over the dark. It is a victory because we're not afraid.

DARK VICTORY [1939]
Humphrey Bogart & Bette Davis

FILM FACT: According to studio publicity this was Bette Davis' personal favorite film. One thing is certain; Humphrey Bogart has perhaps the worst Irish accent ever captured on film.

My heart is a bargain today.
Will you take it?

W.C. Fields

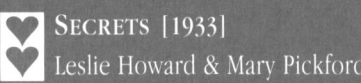
SECRETS [1933]
Leslie Howard & Mary Pickford

FILM FACT: Secrets marked Mary Pickford's retirement from a brilliant screen career.

A woman unsatisfied must have luxuries.
But a woman who loves a man
would sleep on a board.

D.H. Lawrence

 THE SON OF THE SHEIK [1926]
Rudolph Valentino & Vilma Banky

FILM FACT: There has been no greater male screen idol than Rudolph Valentino. The reaction to his premature death was monumental. Although it was believed by many at the time that he had been poisoned by a cast-off mistress, he reportedly died from the effects of a perforated ulcer, possibly aggravated by the extent of his debts.

RICK BLAINE: Here's looking at you, kid.

CASABLANCA [1942]
Humphrey Bogart & Ingrid Bergman

FILM FACT: "I never knew how the picture was going to end, if I was really in love with my husband or Bogart. So I had no idea how I should play the character. I kept begging them to give me the ending, but they'd say: 'We haven't made up our minds. We'll shoot it both ways.' We did the first ending, and they said, 'That's good, we won't bother with the other.'"
—Ingrid Bergman.

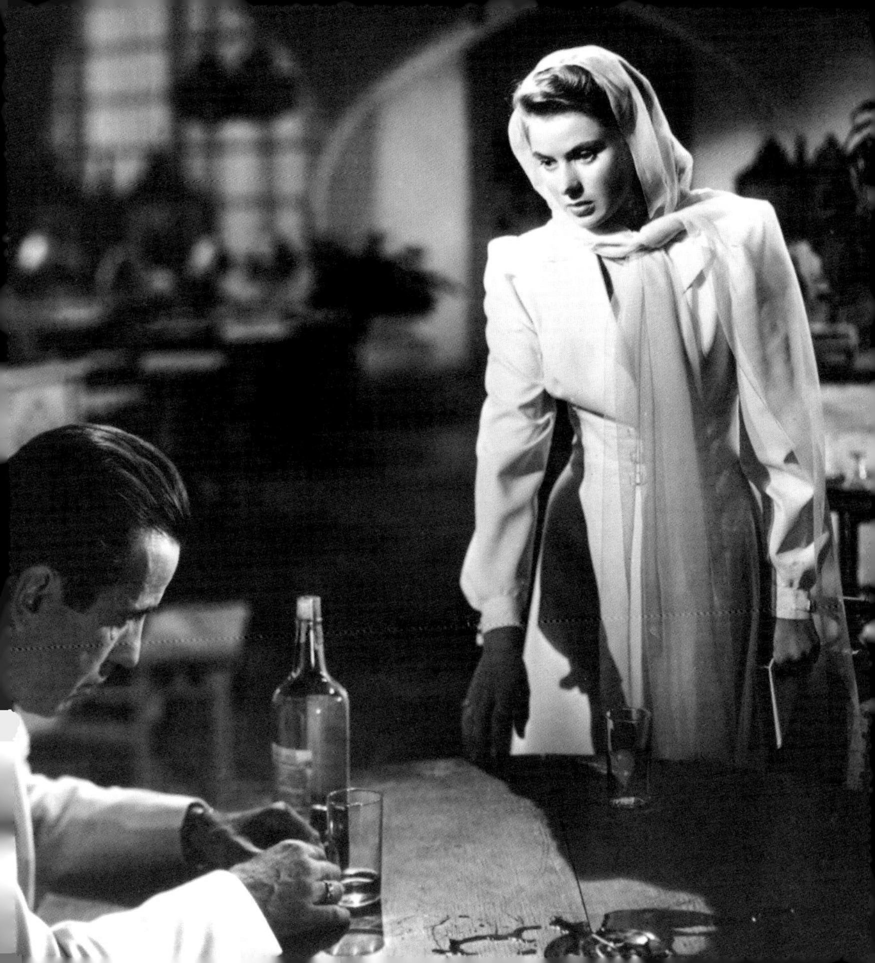

The woman's vision is deep and reaching, the man's far reaching. With the man the world is his heart, with the woman, the heart is her world.

Betty Grable

GIANT [1956]
James Dean & Elizabeth Taylor

FILM FACT: This was James Dean's last film. He crashed his car and died only a couple of weeks after filming ended; his voice is dubbed in several scenes by his good friend, actor Nick Adams.

37

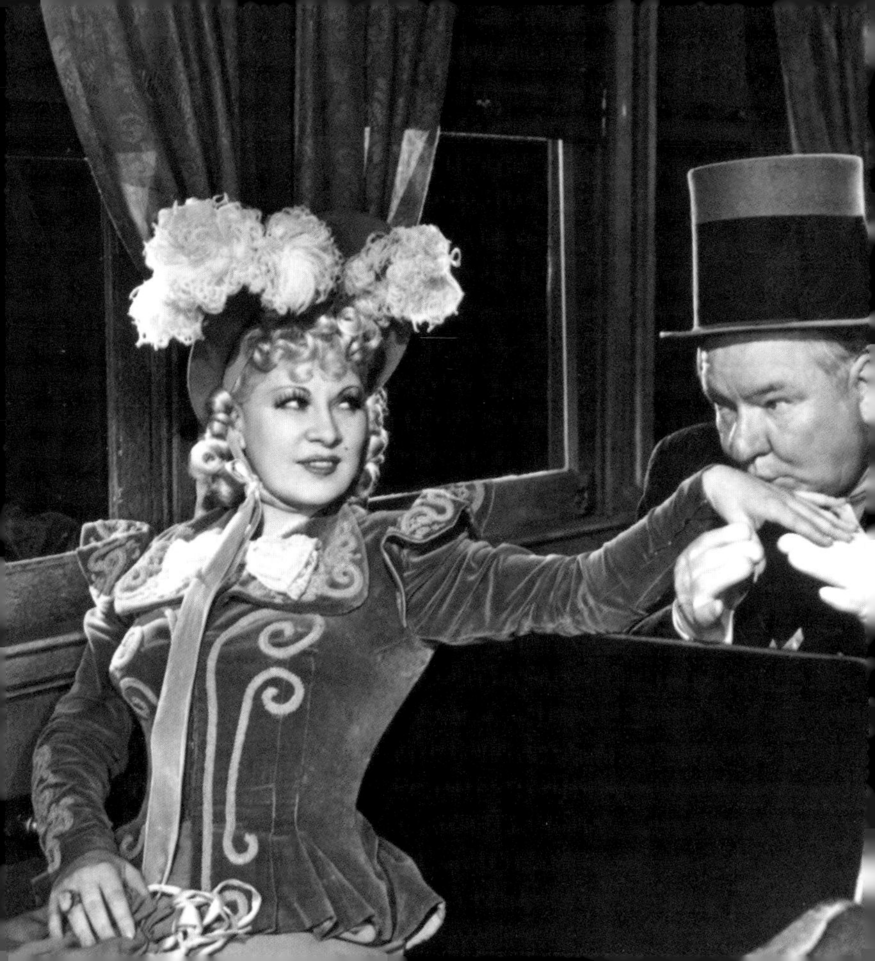

With men he can be rational and unaffected, but when he has ladies to please, every feature works.

Jane Austen

♥ MY LITTLE CHICKADEE [1939]
♥ W.C. Fields & Mae West

FILM FACT: It was no secret that Mae West and W.C. Fields disliked each other intensely, a fact that had an injurious effect on some of their scenes together.

Do not forsake me oh my darling.

Sung by Tex Ritter in High Noon

♥ HIGH NOON [1952]
♥ Gary Cooper & Grace Kelly

FILM FACT: Cooper suffered throughout the filming from a bleeding ulcer and injured hip. It gave him the agonized look that Zinnerman was looking for in his character. Cooper's response when filming ended was, "I'm all acted out."

41

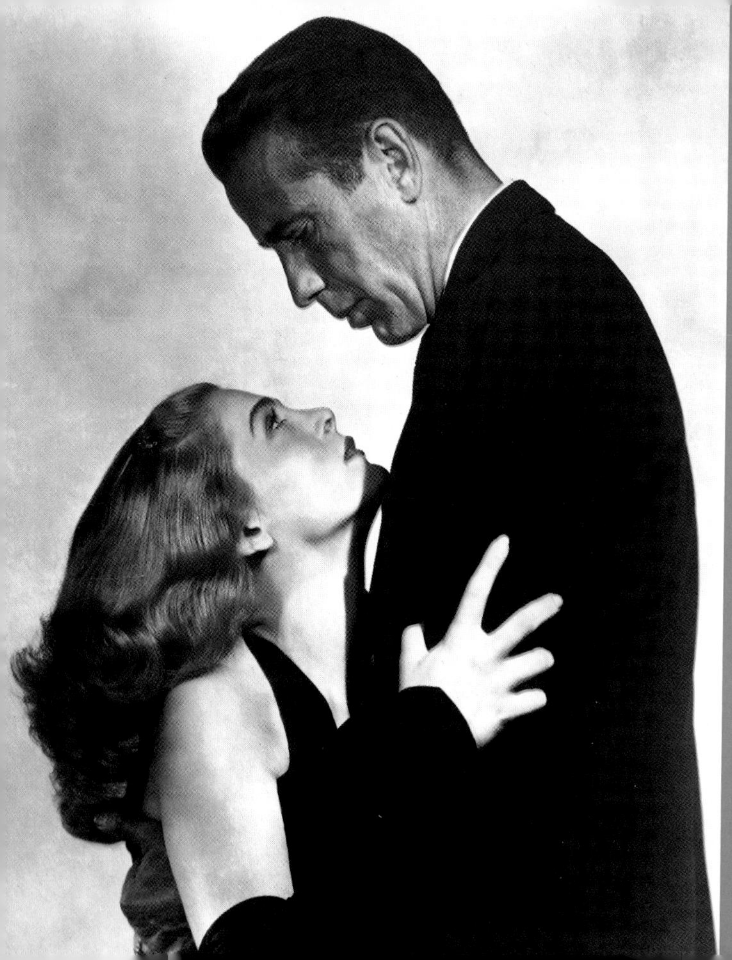

CAPTAIN WARREN "RIP" MURDOCH:
Maybe she was all right, and maybe Christmas comes in July.

♥ **DEAD RECKONING [1947]**
Humphrey Bogart & Lizabeth Scott

FILM FACT: The genuine sexual chemistry that existed between Bacall and Bogart in *The Big Sleep* and *To Have and Have Not* was impossible to emulate in this pairing with Lauren's look-alike Lizabeth Scott. They looked good on screen together but that's about as deep as it got.

Words are only painted fire;
a look is the fire itself.

Mark Twain

♥ **DESTRY RIDES AGAIN** [1939]
♥ James Stewart & Marlene Dietrich

FILM FACT: The incredible catfight between Dietrich and Una Merkel in the film has never been bettered.

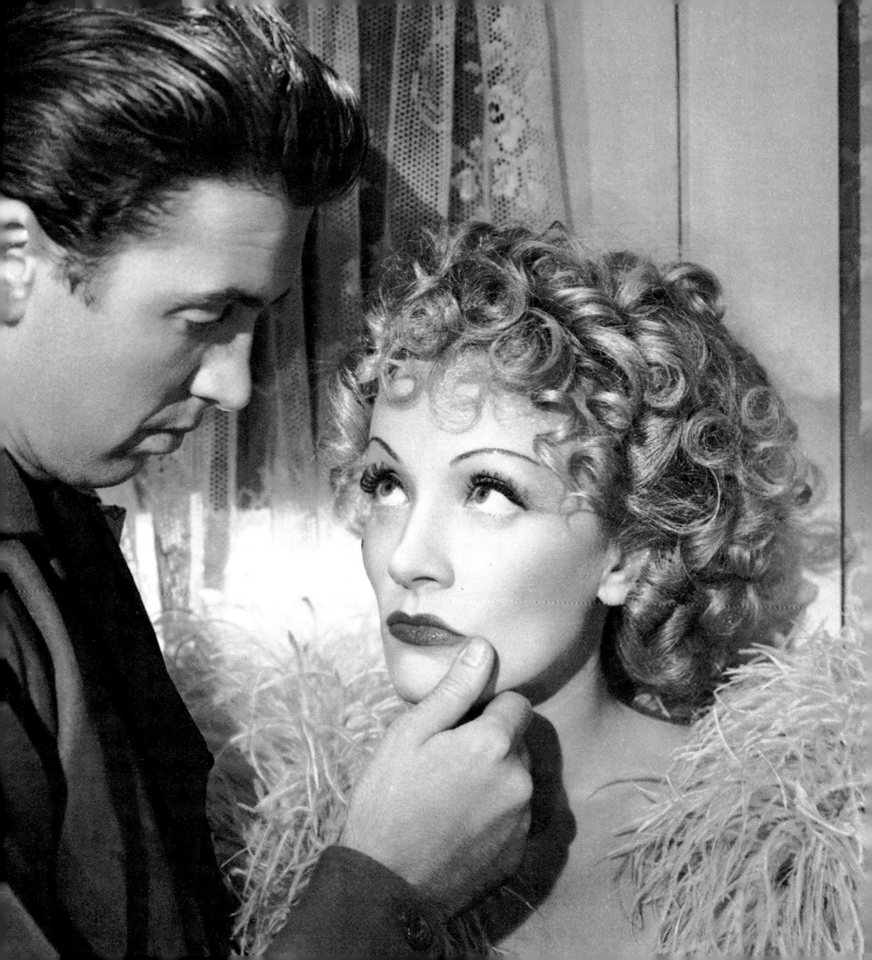

46

We must act out passion before we can feel it.

Jean-Paul Sartre

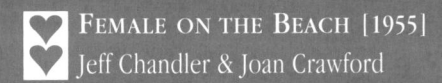

♥ FEMALE ON THE BEACH [1955]
Jeff Chandler & Joan Crawford

FILM FACT: In 1954, Joan was dating, and eluding the marriage proposals of, the president of Universal Studios, when he offered her the role in this film. She was given a royal welcome at Universal and presented with her choice of leading man—Jeff Chandler.

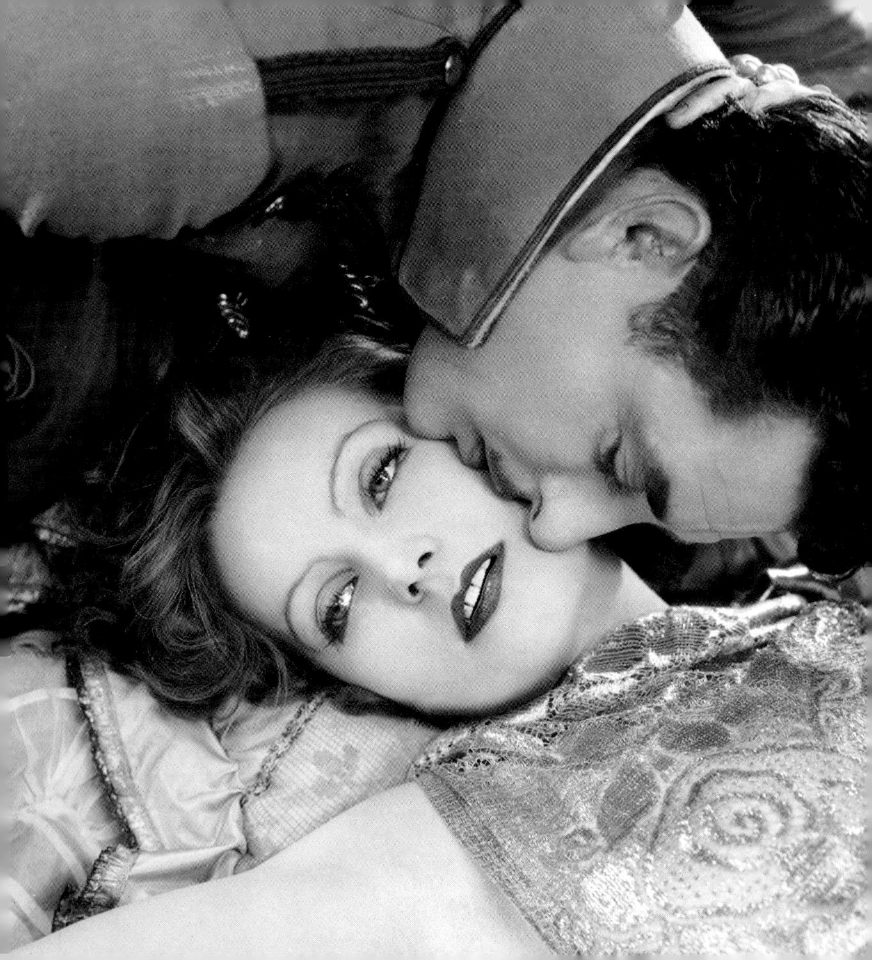

Love seeketh not itself to please, nor for itself hath any care, but for another gives its ease, and builds a Heaven in Hell's despair.

William Blake

♥♥ FLESH AND THE DEVIL [1926]
John Gilbert & Greta Garbo

FILM FACT: Theirs was more than a movie romance. Together Gilbert and Garbo went on to make an adaptation of Tolstoy's *Anna Karenina* titled *Love*. The couple were to marry, but Garbo didn't turn up for the wedding.

When you deal a fast shuffle…
love is in the cards.

♥♥ THE LADY EVE [1941]
Henry Fonda & Barbara Stanwyck

FILM FACT: This classic screwball romantic comedy perfectly paired Barbara Stanwyck in her first true comic role, opposite Henry Fonda, whose down-to-earth performance is absolutely necessary to allow Stanwyck's "saucy woman" delivery to shine.

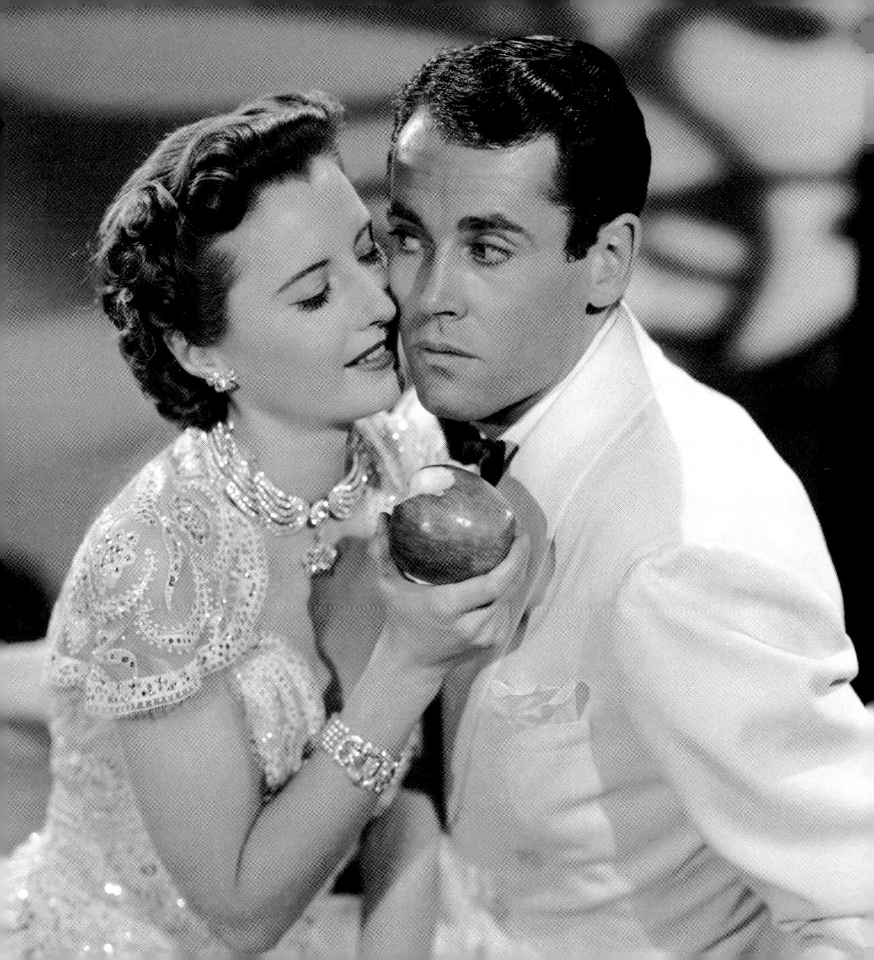

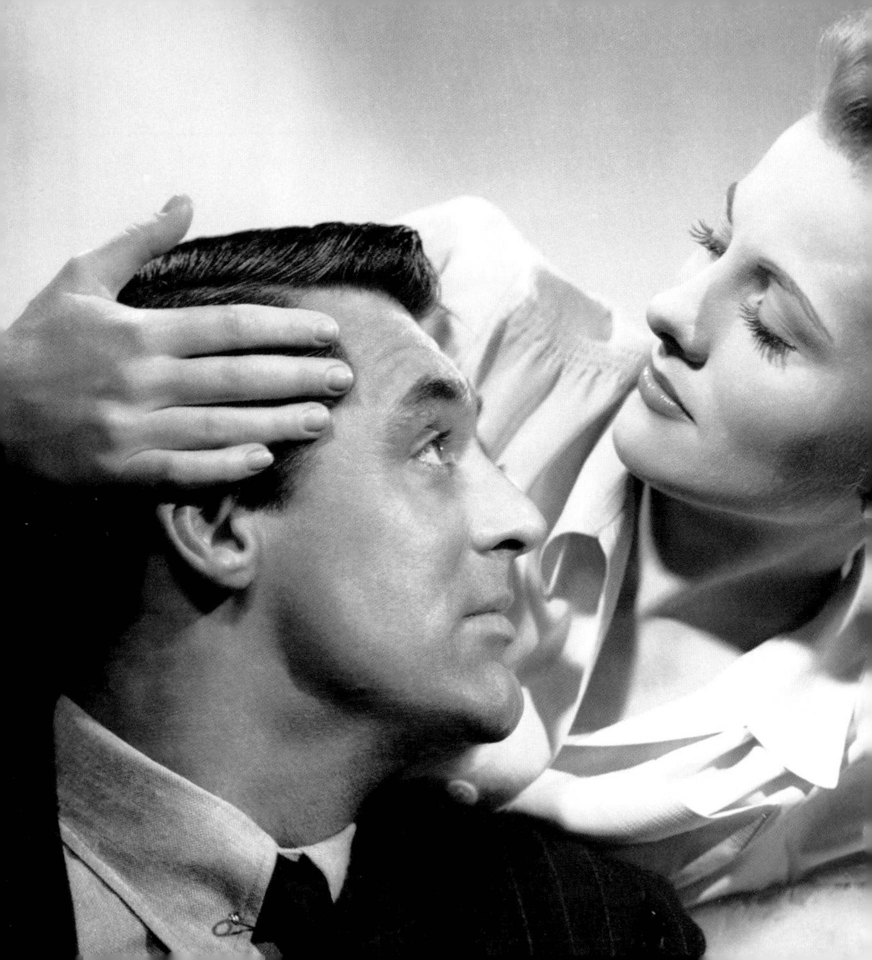

> It is strange what a man may do, and a woman yet think him an angel.
>
> *William M. Thackeray*

♥ SUSPICION [1941]
♥ Cary Grant & Joan Fontaine

FILM FACT: The pair had played together two years earlier in the 1939 movie *Gunga Din*.

Age cannot wither her, nor custom stale her infinite variety. Other women cloy the appetites they feed, but she makes hungry where most she satisfies.

William Shakespeare
Anthony & Cleopatra, *Act II, Scene Two*

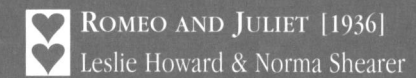

♥♥ ROMEO AND JULIET [1936]
Leslie Howard & Norma Shearer

FILM FACT: Somehow, this Hollywood pairing worked so well that it didn't seem to cross anybody's mind that both of them were far too old to play the leading roles.

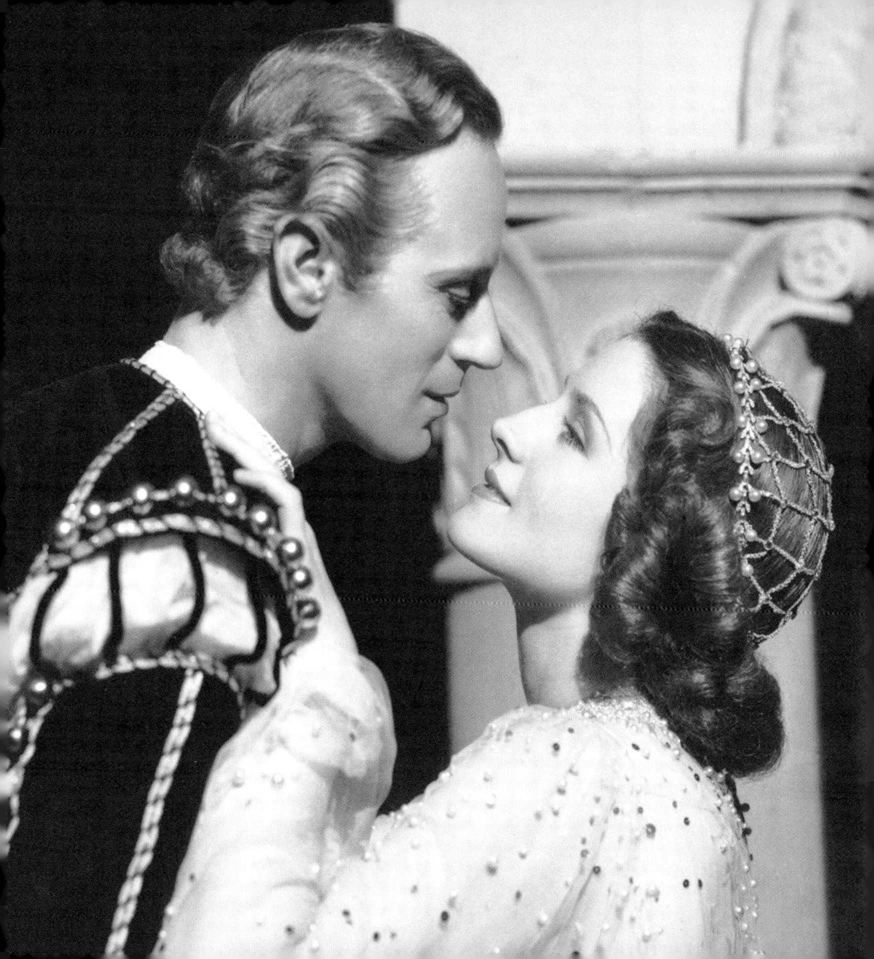

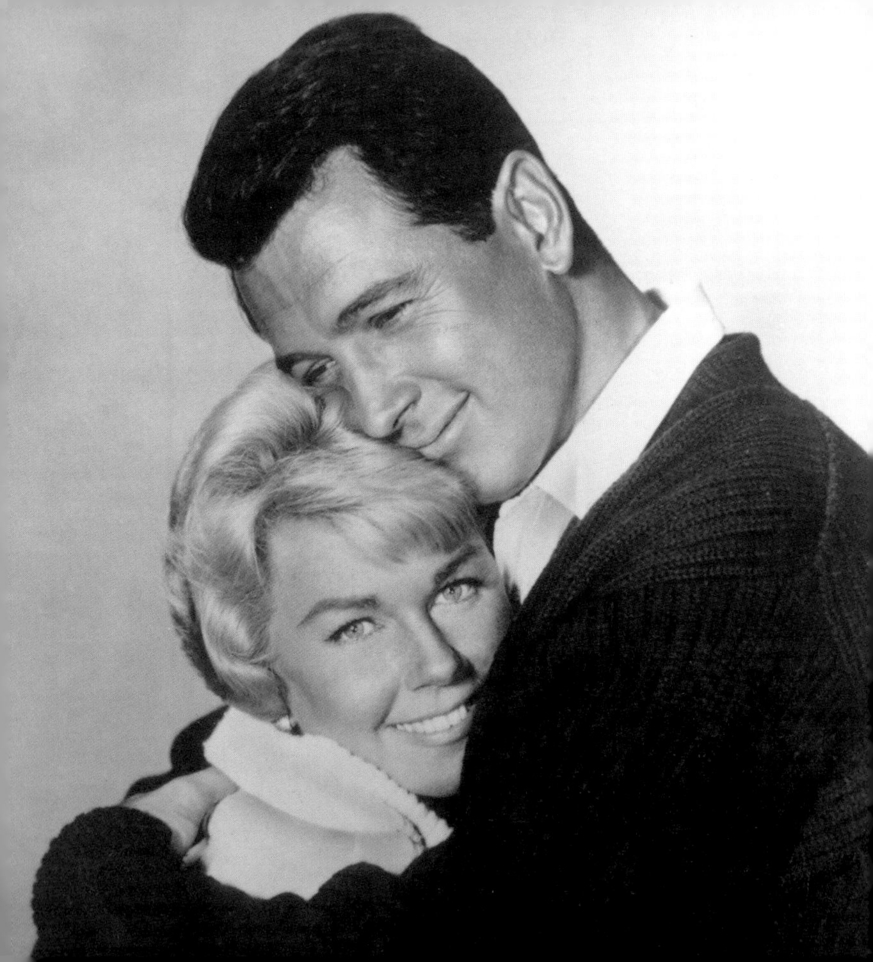

Is it possible that blondes prefer gentlemen?

Mamie van Doren

♥ PILLOW TALK [1959]
Rock Hudson & Doris Day

FILM FACT: This rather silly film allowed Doris Day to shake off the cute image she'd been branded with, and have a somewhat more sexually alluring persona. It worked well, and she and Hudson were among the most popular Hollywood stars for several years to follow.

I love the idea of there being two sexes, don't you?

James Thurber

♥♥ THE QUIET MAN [1952]
John Wayne & Maureen O'Hara

FILM FACT: This film was certainly a family affair, with Wayne's children, O'Hara's brothers, and director John Ford's own kinfolk making up the cast on this heartfelt tribute to the Emerald Isle.

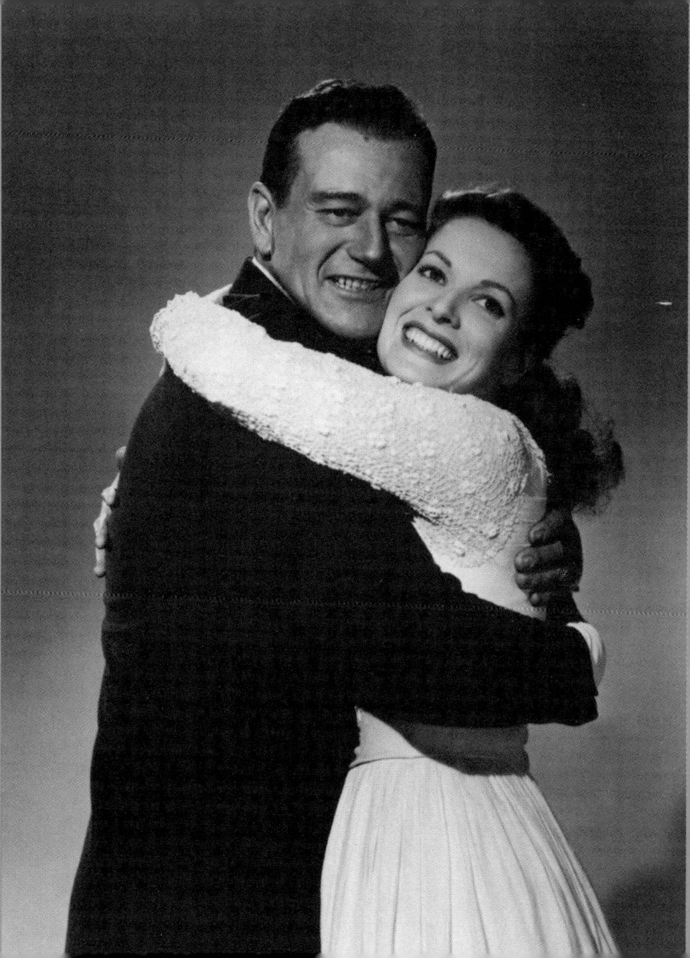

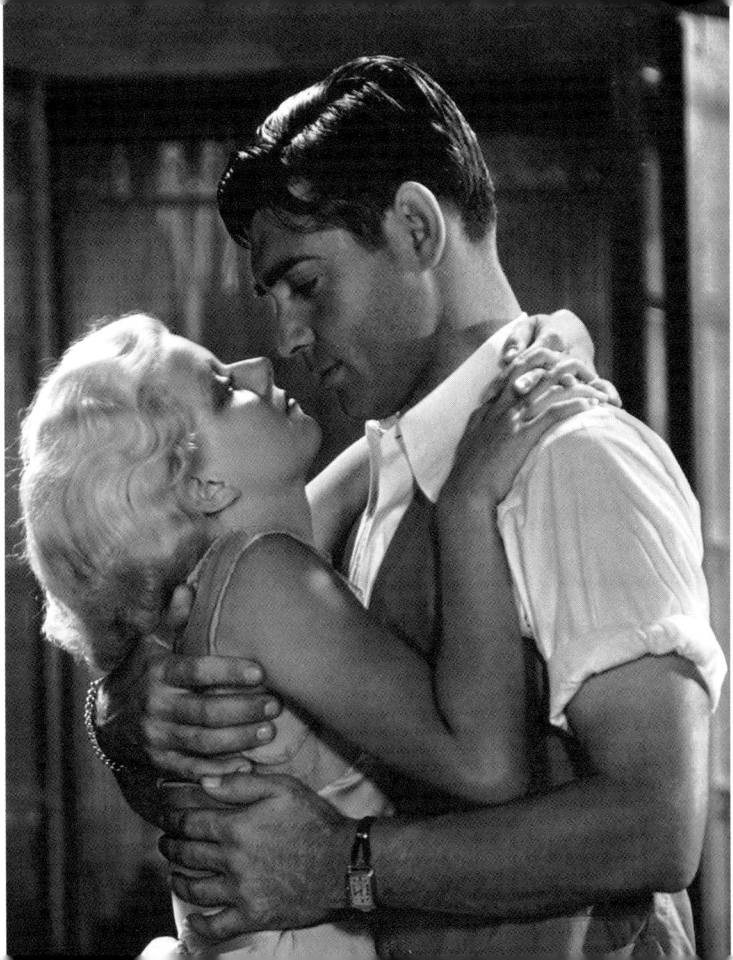

In short I will part with anything for you but you.

Lady Mary Wortley Montagu

RED DUST [1932]
Clark Gable & Jean Harlow

FILM FACT: Fairly "hot" by pre-code standards, *Red Dust* has gained legendary status thanks to Jean Harlow's famous bathing scene in a barrel. According to rumors, footage still exists of her totally nude.

Love is the same as like, except you feel sexier.

Judith Viorst

♥♥ On the Waterfront [1954]
Marlon Brando & Eva Marie Saint

FILM FACT: Inspired by the McCarthy witch hunts, the movie scooped eight Oscars, and Brando was awarded his for best actor, making him the youngest winner at the time.

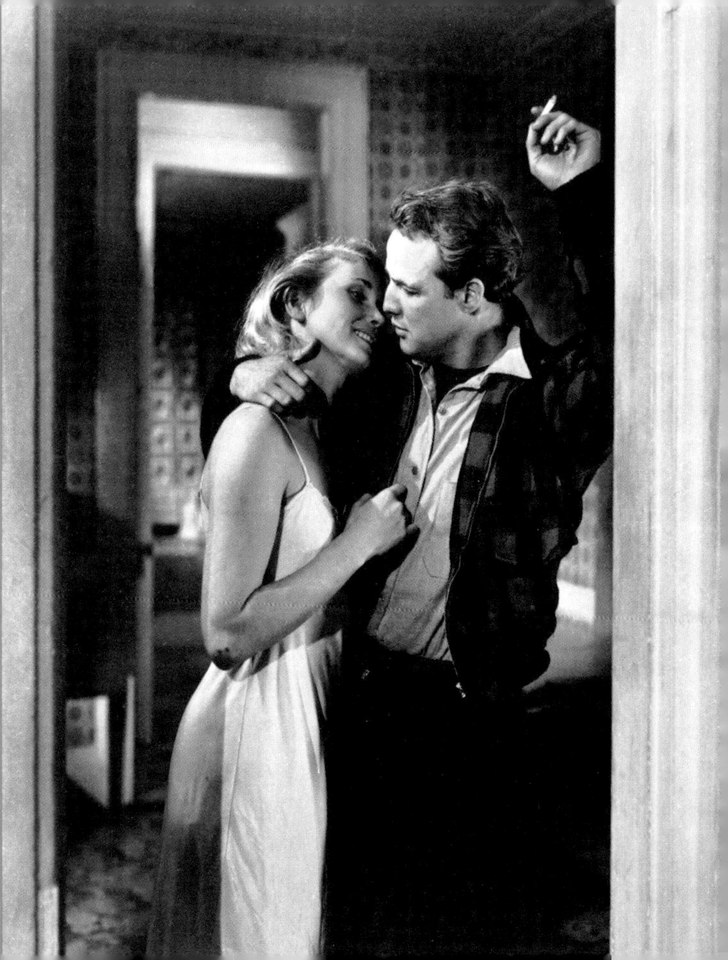

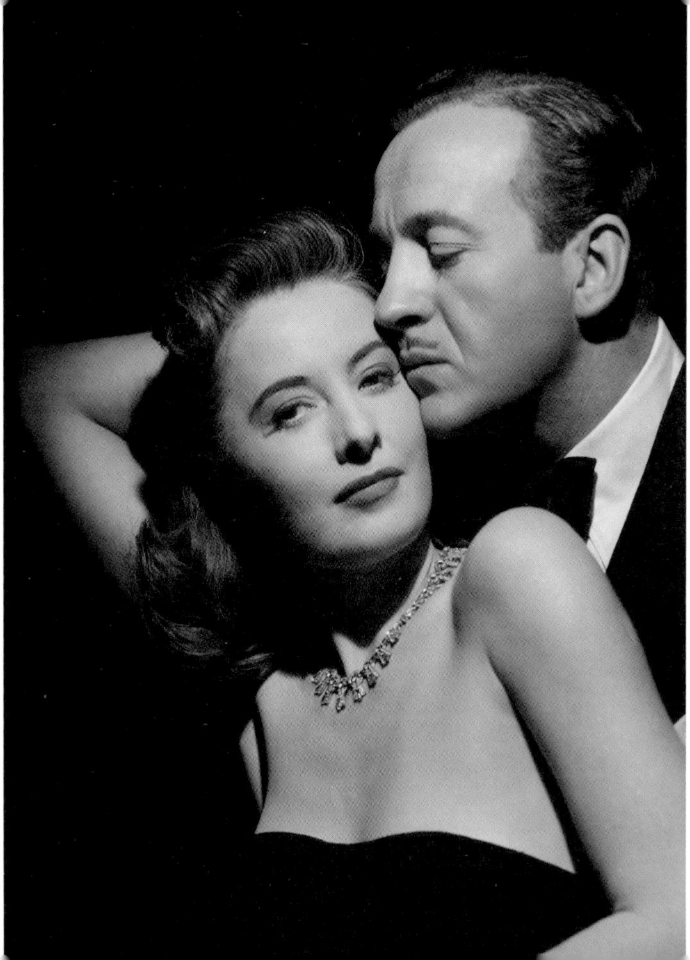

Love is the irresistible desire to
be desired irresistibly.

Louis Ginsberg

♥♥ THE OTHER LOVE [1947]
David Niven & Barbara Stanwyck

FILM FACT: Niven was considered by most as being too lightweight to be a major name, while the IRS had Stanwyck ranked as America's highest-earning woman…not bad for a girl orphaned at the age of four and raised by her showgirl sister.

No one worth possessing can
be quite possessed.

Sara Teasdale

♥♥ BEVERLY OF GRAUSTARK [1926]
Antonio Moreno & Marion Davies

FILM FACT: Antonio Moreno's waning career was revitalized by the wave of demand for on-screen Latin Lovers that followed the arrival of Rudolph Valentino.

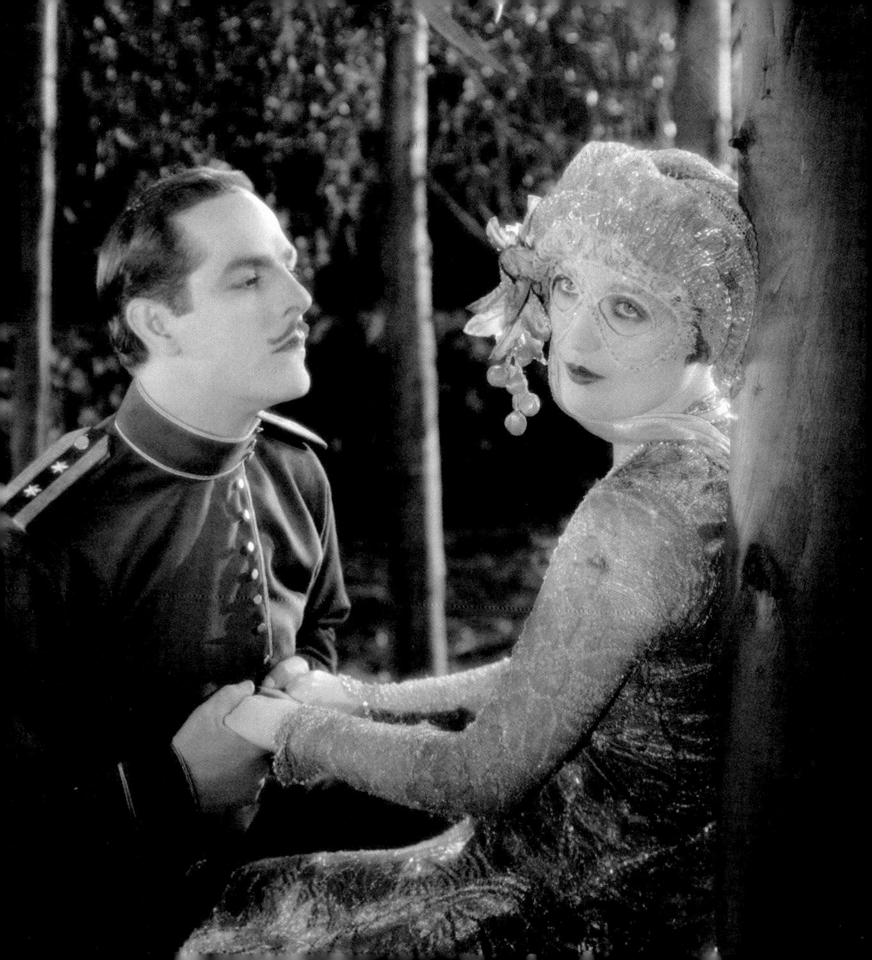

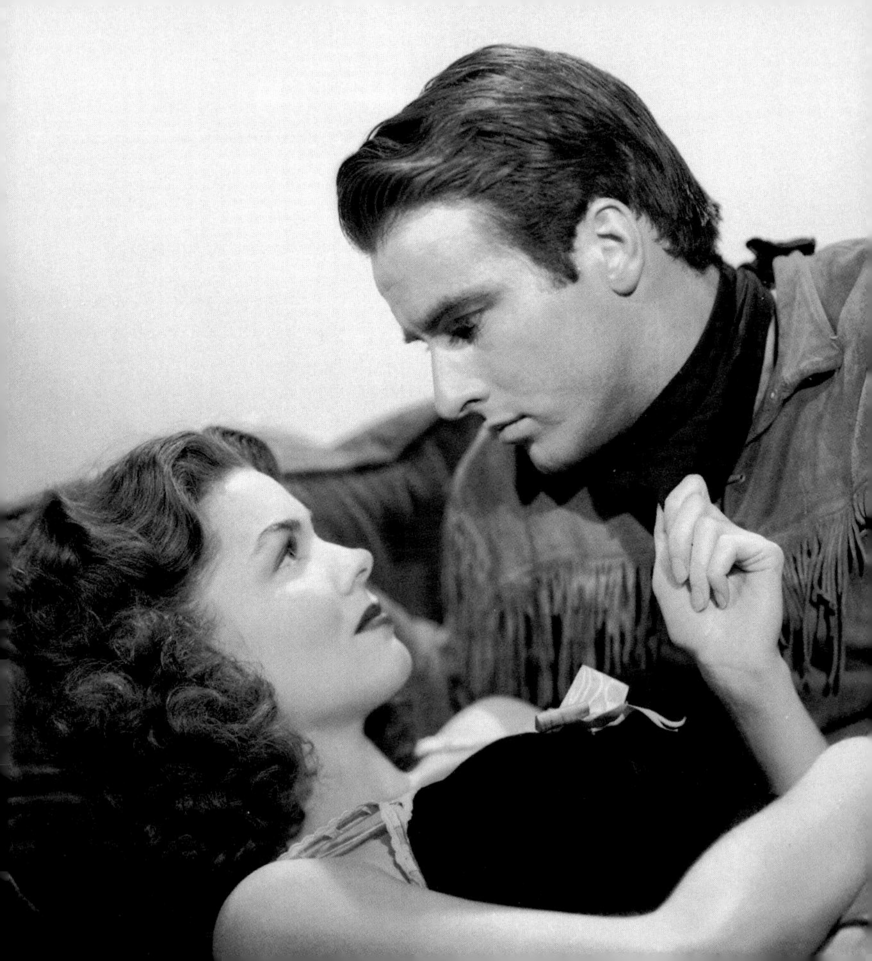

Love is lost in men's
capricious minds,
but in women's, it fills
all the room it finds.

John Crowne

♥ RED RIVER [1948]
♥ Montgomery Clift & Joanne Dru

FILM FACT: John Ireland, who was cast in the film as Cherry Valance, fell in love with Joanne Dru during filming, and they were married shortly afterward. In his movie debut, it was also the beginning of a beautiful relationship for Clift with the camera, which instantly loved him.

Rose: Dear...what is your first name?
Charlie: Charlie.
Rose: Charlie...that's a nice name... Charlie... Charlie...
Charlie: Give us a kiss.

♥ African Queen [1951]
♥ Humphrey Bogart & Katharine Hepburn

Film Fact: Bogart and Hepburn achieved some of the strongest acting ever captured on film, yet, curiously, this was their only pairing together.

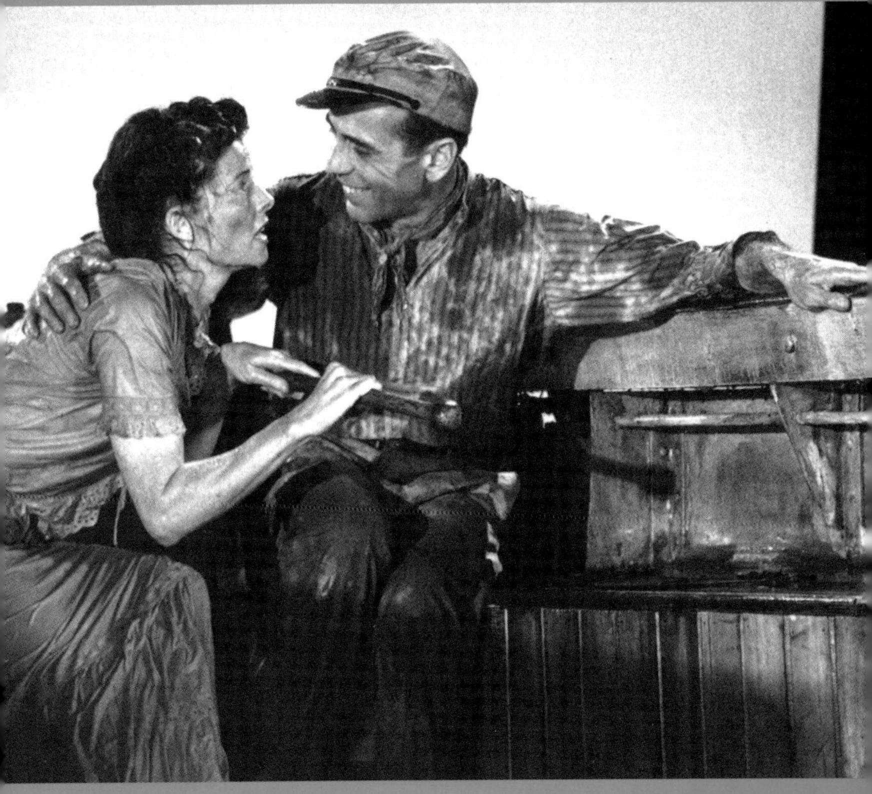

Where love is concerned,
too much is not enough.

Pierre de Beaumarchais
Marriage of Figaro, *1784*

GILDA [1946]
Glenn Ford & Rita Hayworth

FILM FACT: Rita Hayworth, who had a capacity to be more provocative on screen than any other actress of the time, blamed the producer for creating a sex goddess no woman could ever live up to.

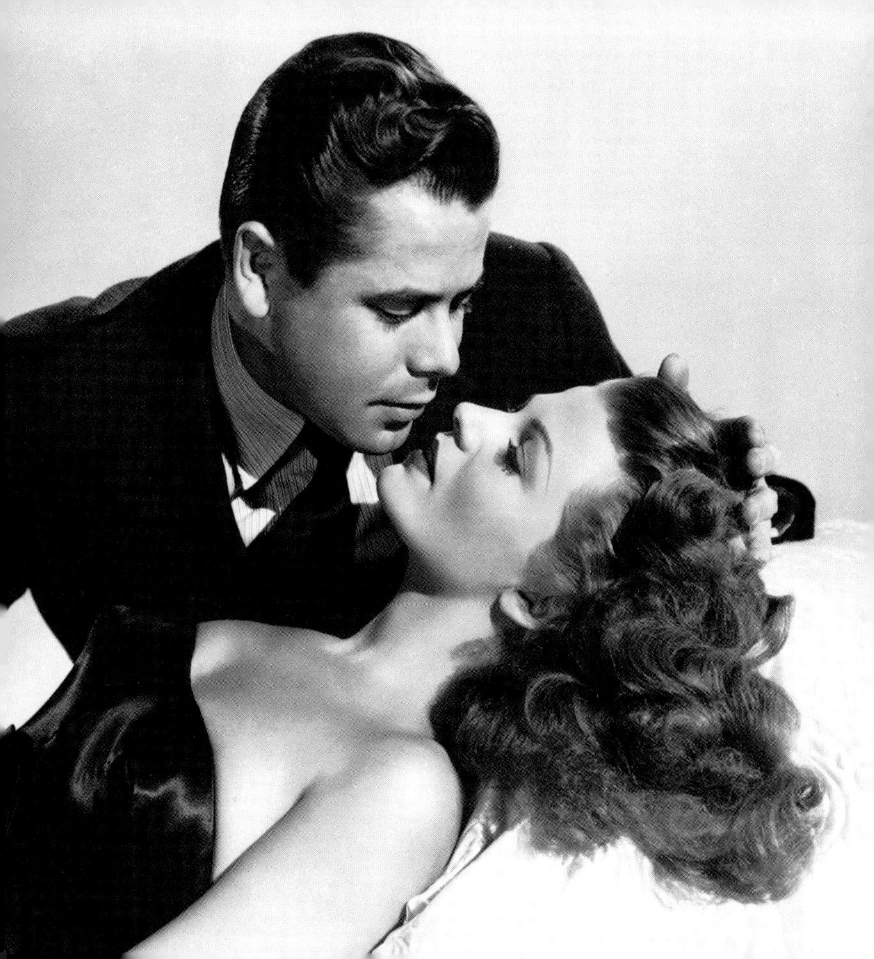

74

In love, there is always one who kisses and one who offers the cheek.

French Proverb

♥ GONE WITH THE WIND [1939]
♥ Clark Gable & Vivien Leigh

FILM FACT: One famous scene is the epic burning of Atlanta, which was achieved by burning a huge wall left over on the backlots from the making of *King Kong*.

Men always want to be a woman's first love.
Women have a more subtle instinct:
What they like is to be a man's last romance.

Oscar Wilde

♥ IVANHOE [1952]
♥ Robert Taylor & Elizabeth Taylor

FILM FACT: Both Taylors turned down the film, but both turned up on the set in England ready to shoot what Elizabeth went on to consider "just a big medieval Western."

77

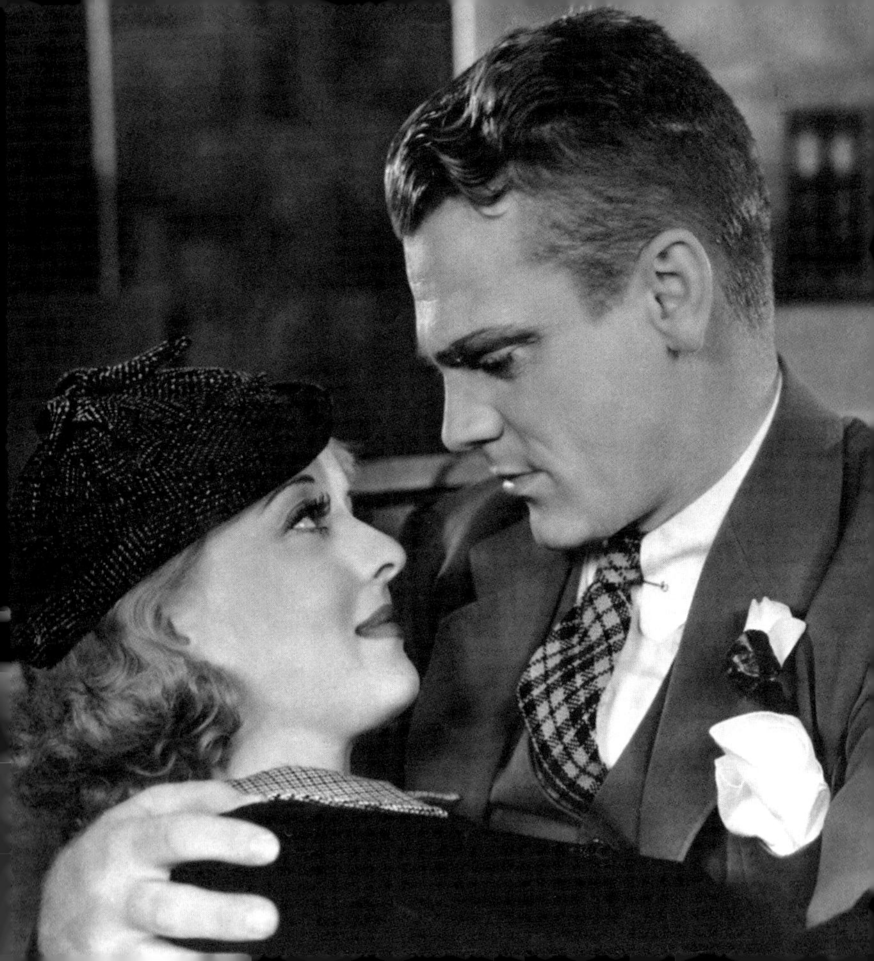

> Don't threaten me with love, baby.
> Let's just go walking in the rain.
>
> *Billie Holiday*

♥♥ JIMMY THE GENT [1934]
James Cagney & Bette Davis

FILM FACT: James Cagney was getting tired of the formula pictures being offered him, so rather than go on suspension, he protested by getting a crewcut, which is how he appears in this film.

Whatever our souls are made of, his and mine are the same.

Emily Brontë

♥♥ MAGNIFICENT OBSESSION [1954]
Rock Hudson & Jayne Wyman

FILM FACT: This is Jayne Wyman's film, as her Oscar nomination for the role reveals. Who would have thought that her ex-husband Ronald Reagan would become president?

81

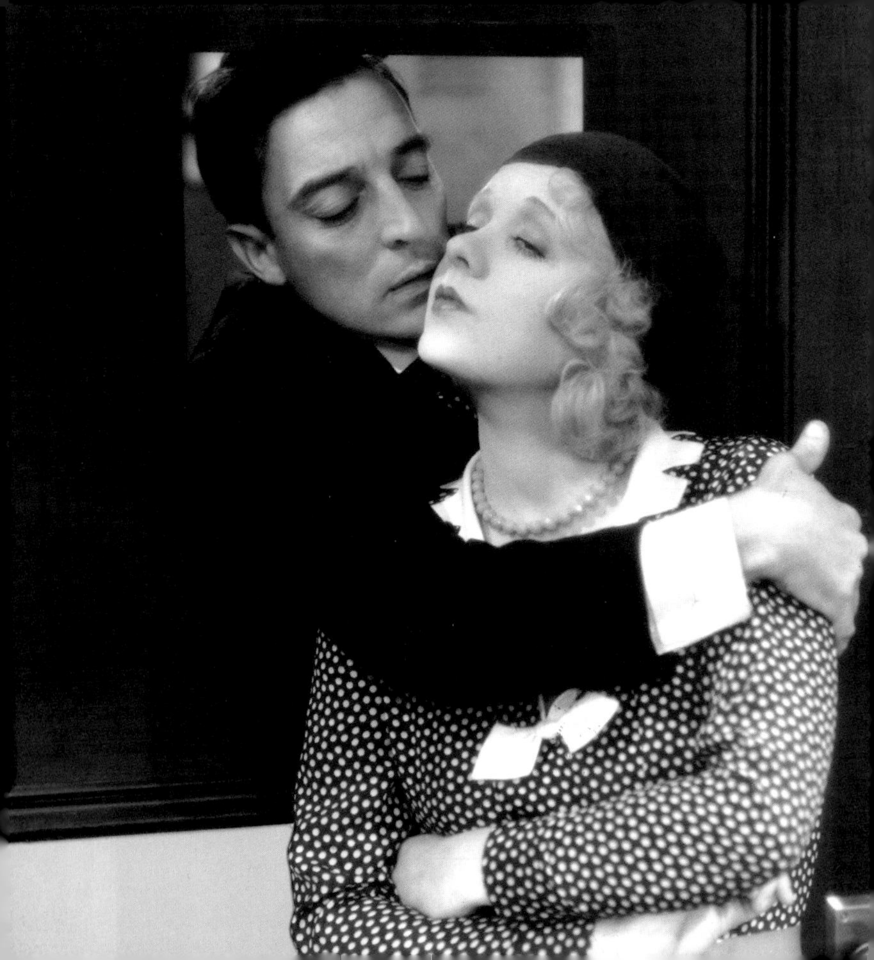

Women like silent men.
They think they're listening.

Marcel Archard

♥♥ SIDEWALKS OF NEW YORK [1931]
Buster Keaton & Anita Page

FILM FACT: Keaton said he knew before the camera turned on the first scene that it was the perfect foundation for a stinker, and so he did what so many others had done: He turned to drink, and that is when he blew it.

It's the kissiest business in
the world. You have to
keep kissing people.

Ava Gardner

♥♥ La Dame aux Camélias [1953]
Roland Alexandre & Micheline Presle

FILM FACT: This time the pair is a pair of movies as Dumas' *La Dame Aux Camelias* was filmed twice in the same year—a modernized adaptation shot in Argentina and a faithful 19th-century version in France with Roland Alexandre and Micheline Presle.

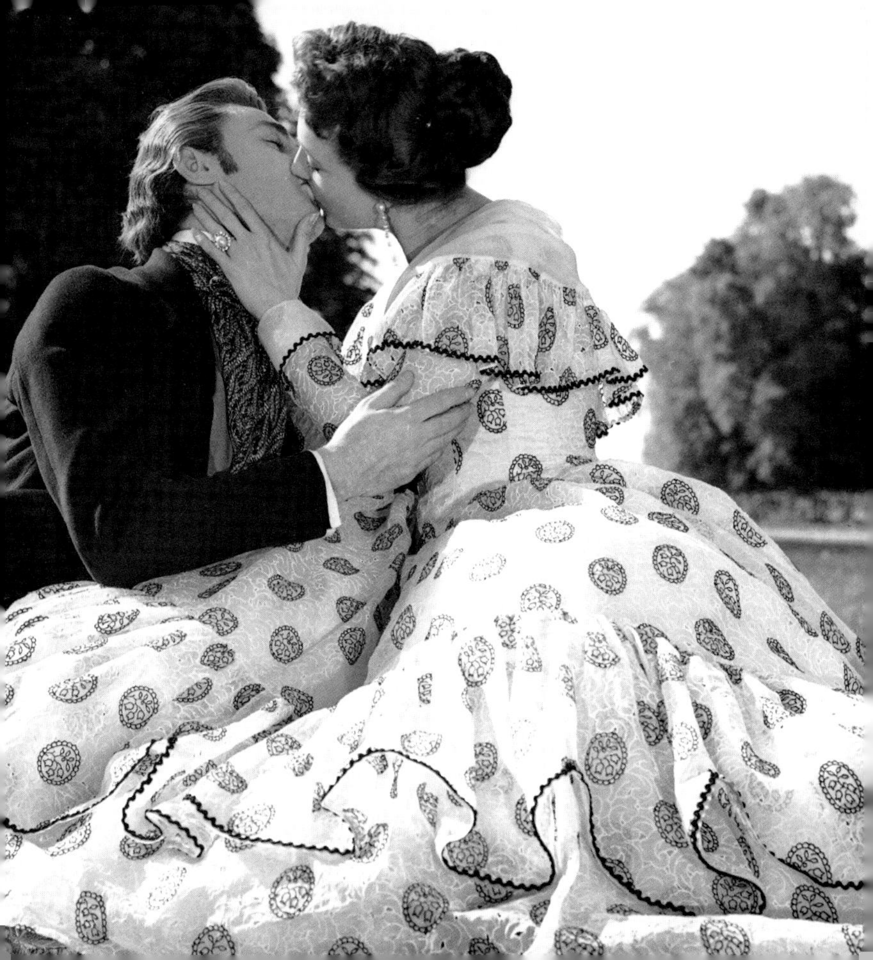

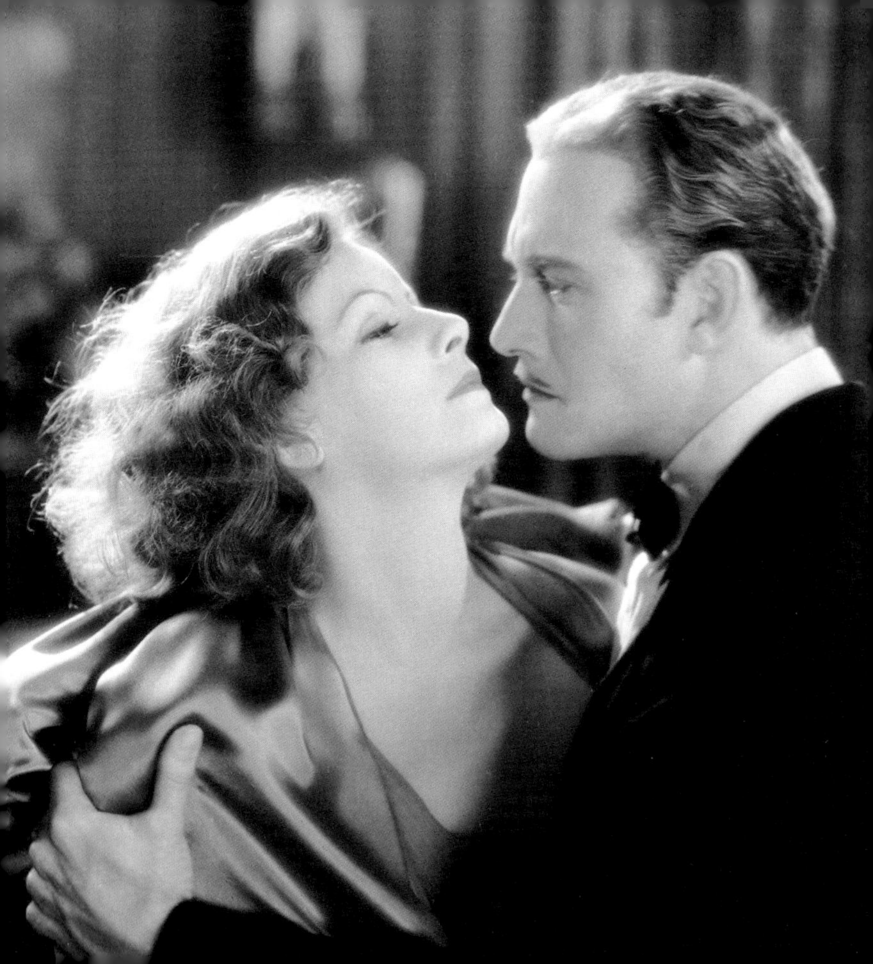

The sweetest joy, the
wildest woe is love.

Pearl Bailey

♥♥ THE MYSTERIOUS LADY [1928]
Conrad Nagel & Greta Garbo

FILM FACT: Garbo's popularity hinged on more than just her sensuality. There was something mysterious about her. She displayed cold stares and harbored a complicated personality, or so it seemed. Her sex appeal, along with some morally questionable storylines, challenged compliance with Will Hays' Production Code more than once.

A kiss is a lovely trick designed by nature to stop speech when words become superfluous.

Ingrid Bergman

♥♥ YOU ONLY LIVE TWICE [1967]
Sean Connery & Mie Hama

FILM FACT: Apparently, due to illness during filming, Mie Hama (Kissy Suzuki) had to be doubled in a diving scene by Diane Cilento, who was Sean Connery's wife at the time.

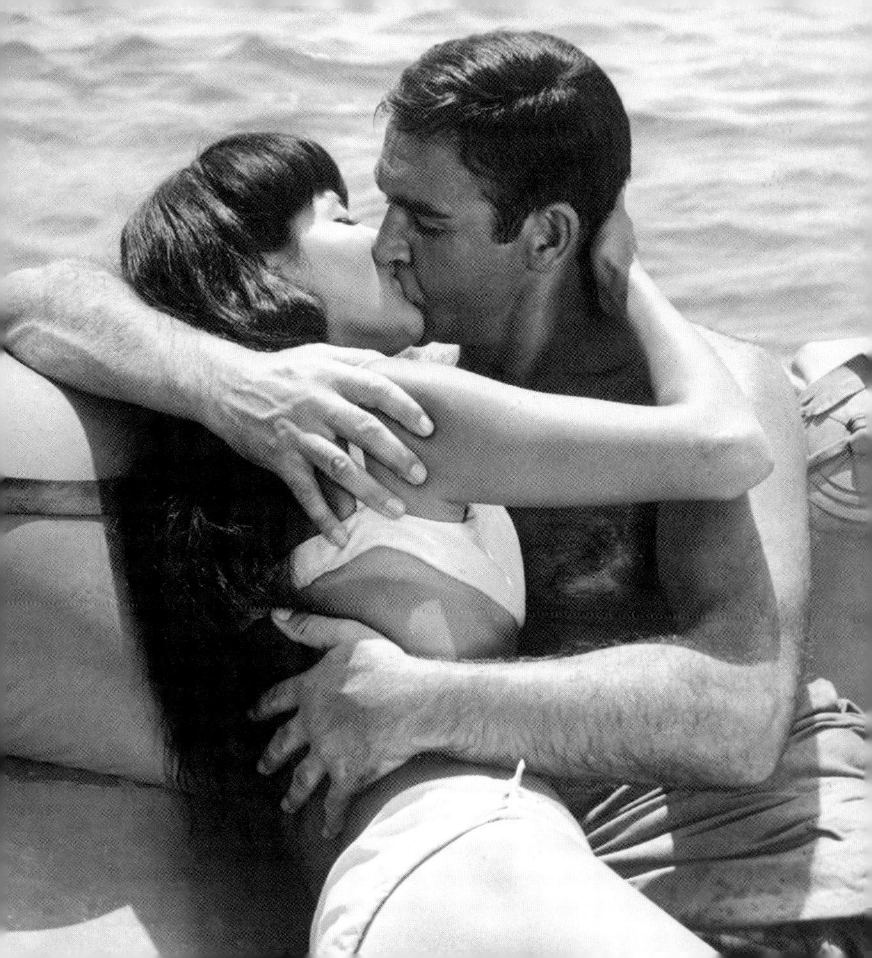

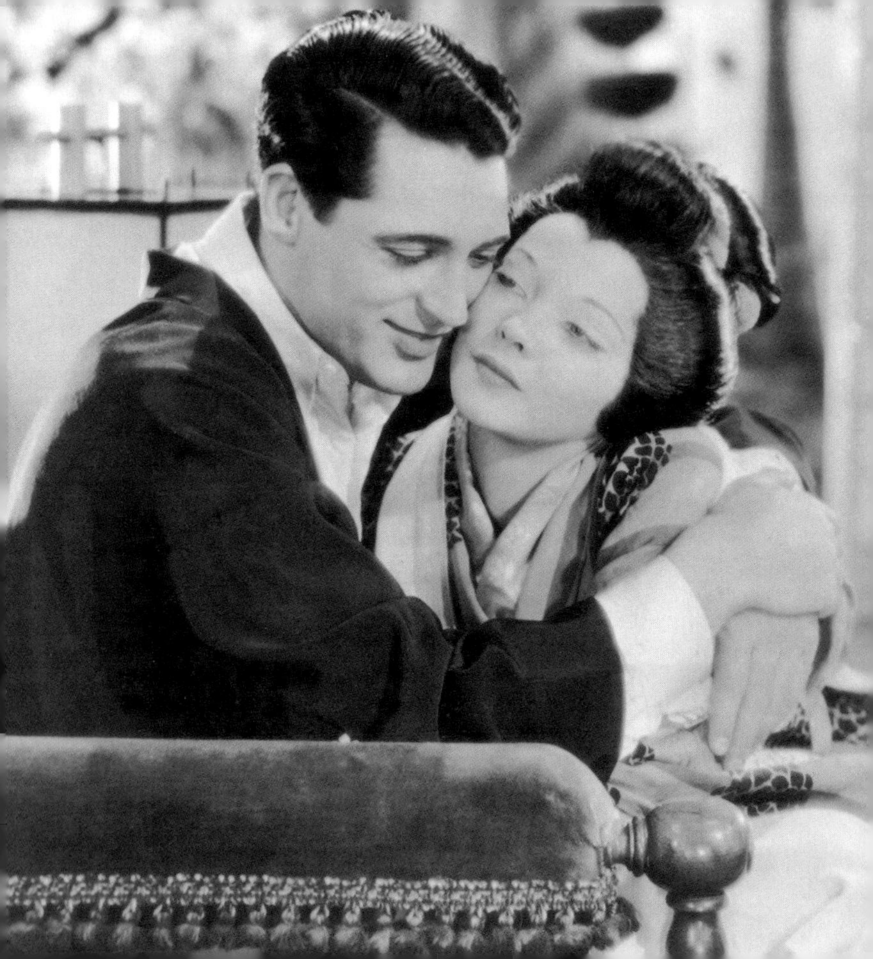

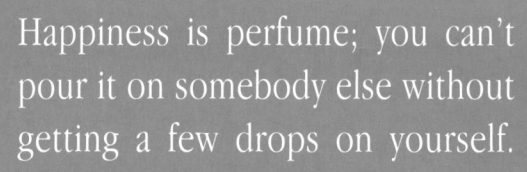

Happiness is perfume; you can't pour it on somebody else without getting a few drops on yourself.

James Van De Zee

♥ **MADAME BUTTERFLY** [1932]
♥ Cary Grant & Sylvia Sidney

FILM FACT: Sylvia Sidney—a New York girl offscreen—is extremely convincing as the Asian heroine Cho Cho San.

Beauty is worse than wine,
it intoxicates both the holder
and beholder.

Immermann

♥♥ SABRINA [1954]
William Holden & Audrey Hepburn

FILM FACT: Because film director Billy Wilder was writing *Sabrina* by night and shooting the next day, Hepburn allegedly conspired to create delays on the set so that Wilder could have more time.

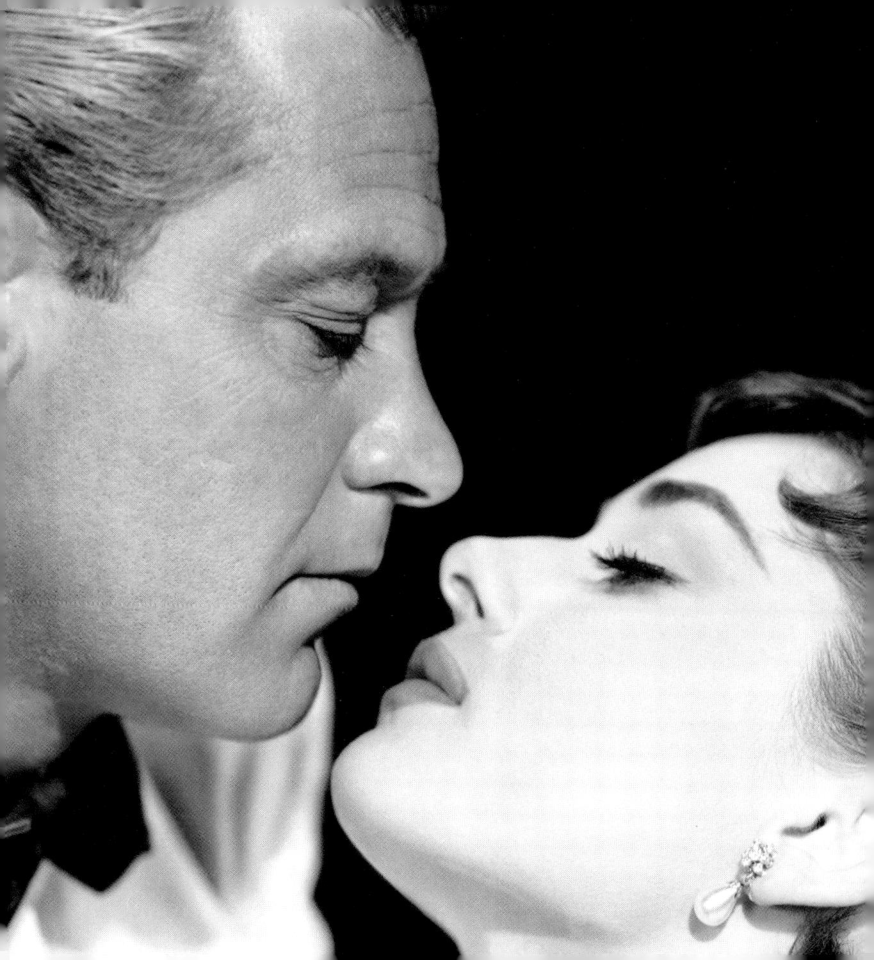

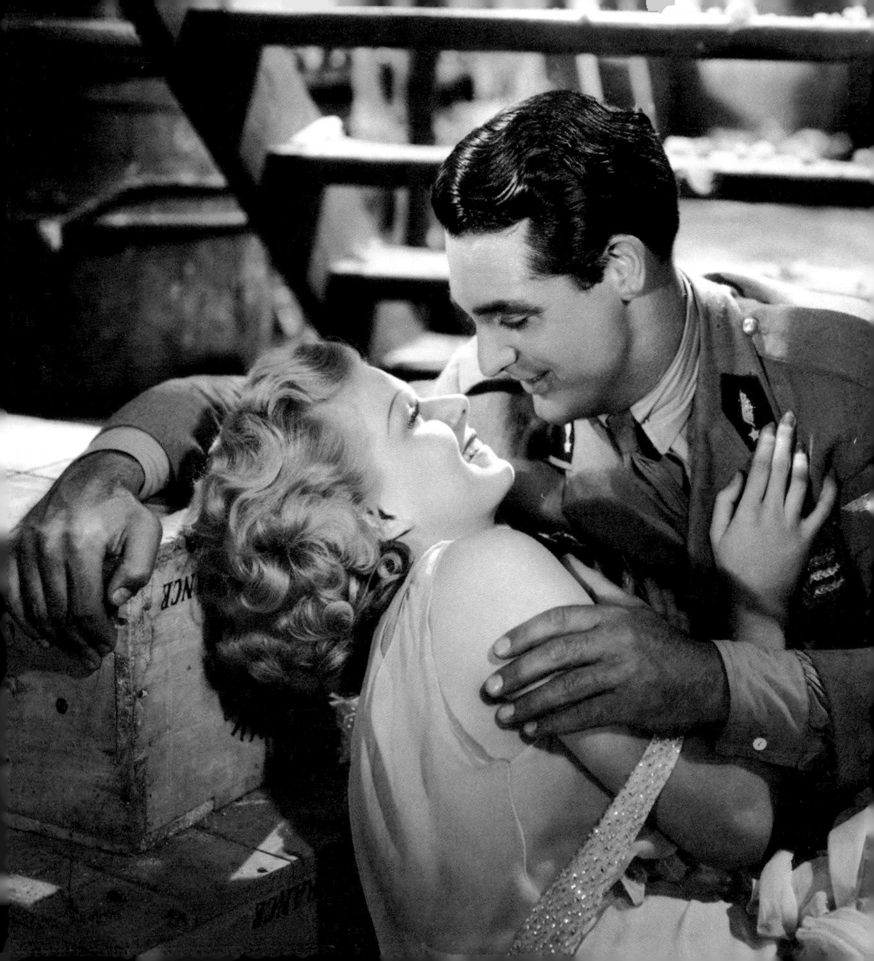

The most precious possession that ever comes to man in this world is a woman's heart.

J.G. Holland

♥ Suzy [1936]
♥ Cary Grant & Jean Harlow

FILM FACT: It was only in 1935, when Cary Grant managed to free himself from Paramount, that he began to demonstrate his inspired comic flair, and it took being paired with the extremely sexy and funny Jean Harlow to get him to sing a love ballard onscreen.

No woman ever hates a man for being in love with her; but many a woman hates a man for being her friend.

Alexander Pope

♥♥ BRIGHT LEAF [1950]
Gary Cooper & Lauren Bacall

FILM FACT: The smouldering Gary Cooper provided the sizzling Bacall's other half in this film adapted from a slow-burning novel about rival tobacco barons, yet the result was no more than a lukewarm melodrama.

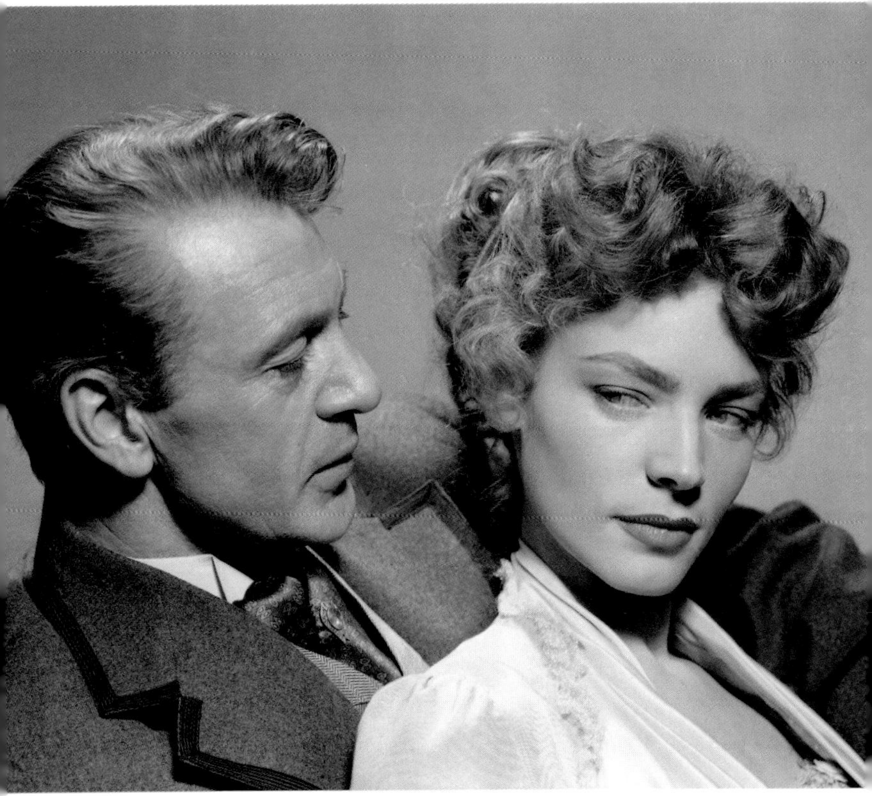

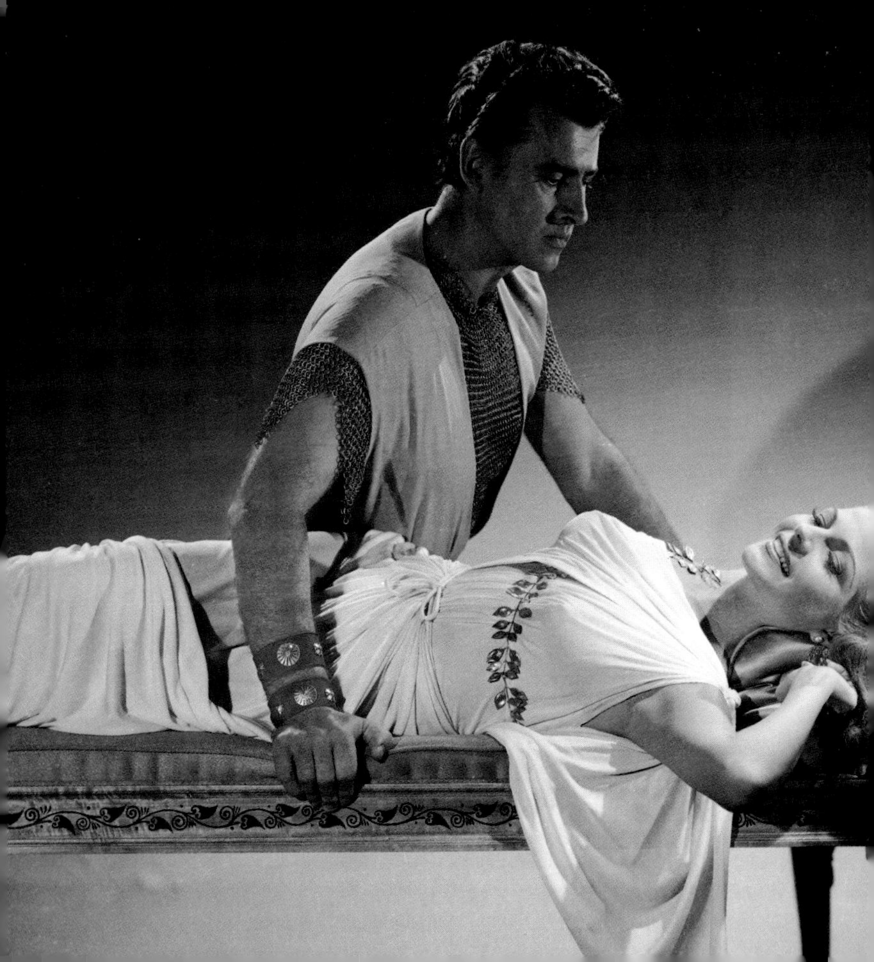

> You are my lover and I am your mistress, and kingdoms and empires and governments have tottered and succumbed before now to that mighty combination.
>
> *Violet Trefuis*

♥ SALOME [1953]
Stewart Granger & Rita Hayworth

FILM FACT: *Salome* was the film Rita Hayworth was pushed into making right after her big "comeback" film, *Affair in Trinidad*. She was tired and needed a break between films. When Columbia studio head Harry Cohn, a man often described as "tyrannical," refused to give her a vacation, she simply didn't show up when filming began on *Salome*. She took her much needed vacation before coming back to work on *Salome*.

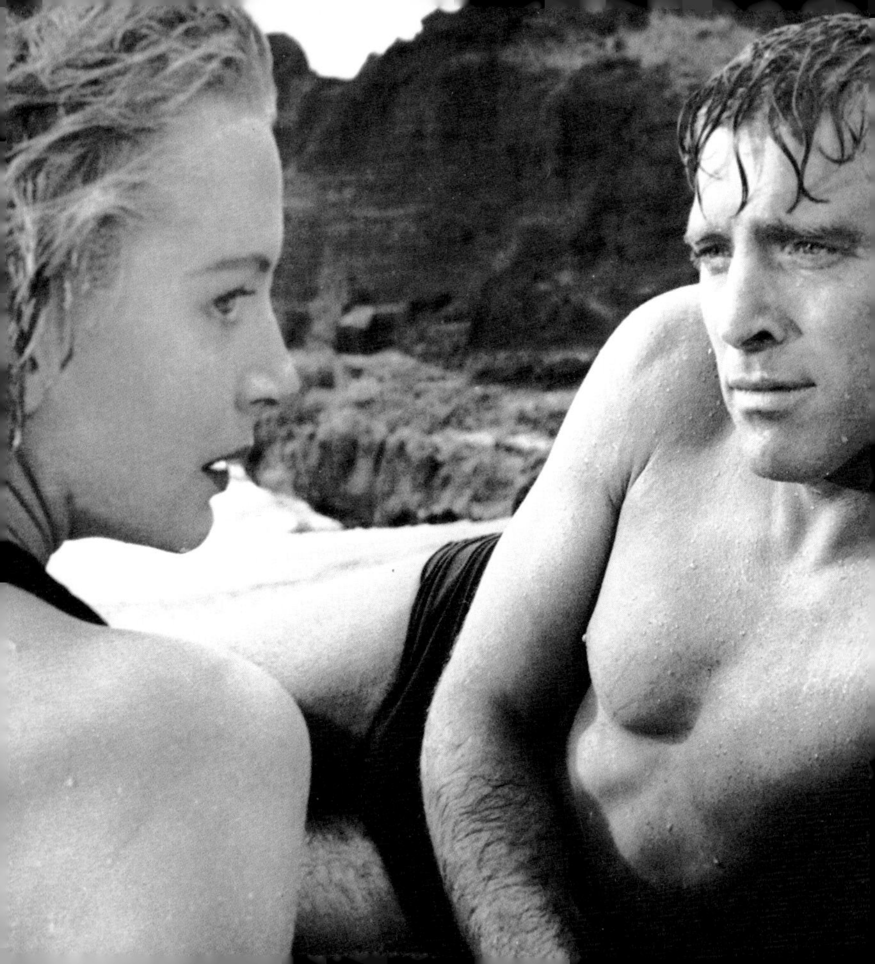

KAREN HOLMES: I never knew it could be like this! Nobody ever kissed me the way you do.
SERGEANT MILTON WARDEN: Nobody?
KAREN HOLMES: No, nobody.

♥♥ FROM HERE TO ETERNITY [1953]
Burt Lancaster & Deborah Kerr

FILM FACT: Joan Crawford was to have played the officer's straying wife, but the part went to Deborah Kerr, whose sway from "ice maiden" to "woman consumed with passion" kept the movie memorably realistic, helping to create one of the most indelible images in film history.

MIMI: It's growing so dark,
Rodolphe…I can't see you…

♥ LA BOHEME [1926]
♥ John Gilbert & Lillian Gish

FILM FACT: John Gilbert was said to be infatuated with Gish and savored making the love scenes during the film, but Gish would have been happier with no love scenes at all. "Oh, dear, I've got to go through another day of kissing John Gilbert," she complained.

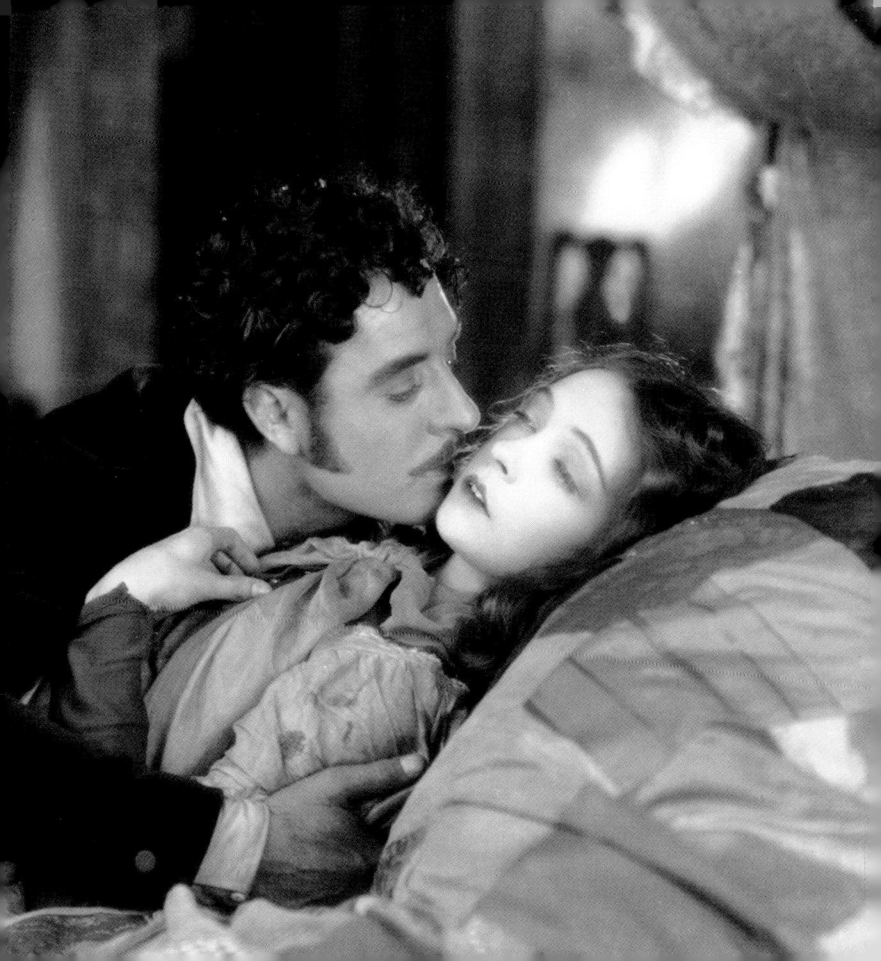

> It is not the size of the
> man, but the size of his
> heart that matters.
>
> *Evander Holyfield*

WITHOUT LOVE [1945]
Spencer Tracy & Katharine Hepburn

FILM FACT: Katharine Hepburn and Spencer Tracy were practically inseparable on the big screen, which is surprising since when they first met, Katharine greeted him with, "I'm afraid that I'm a little tall for you, Mr. Tracy." To which he replied, "Don't worry. I'll soon cut you down to size."

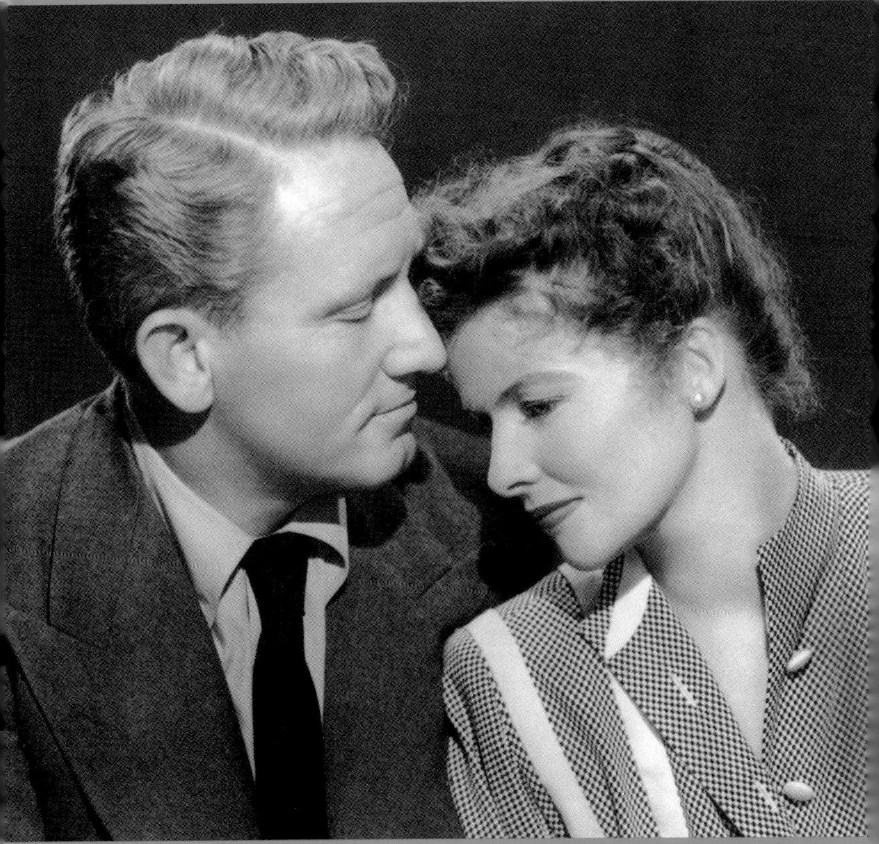

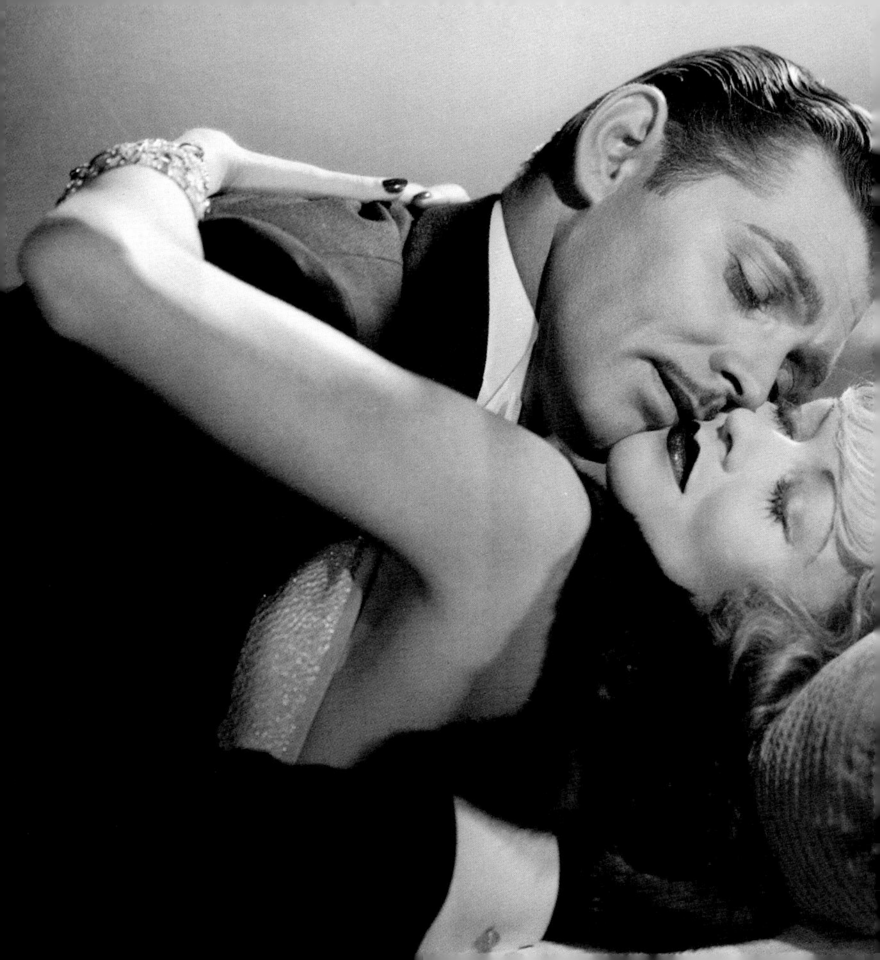

A woman who takes things from a man is called a girlfriend; a man who takes things from a woman is called a gigolo.

Ruthie Stein

♥♥ AFTER OFFICE HOURS [1934]
Clark Gable & Constance Bennett

FILM FACT: Constance Bennett had left the film industry to marry her third husband, the Marquis de la Falaise de la Coudray, a well-known playboy of questionable royal lineage. This unhappy union ended in the early 1930s, and Constance resumed life on the big screen.

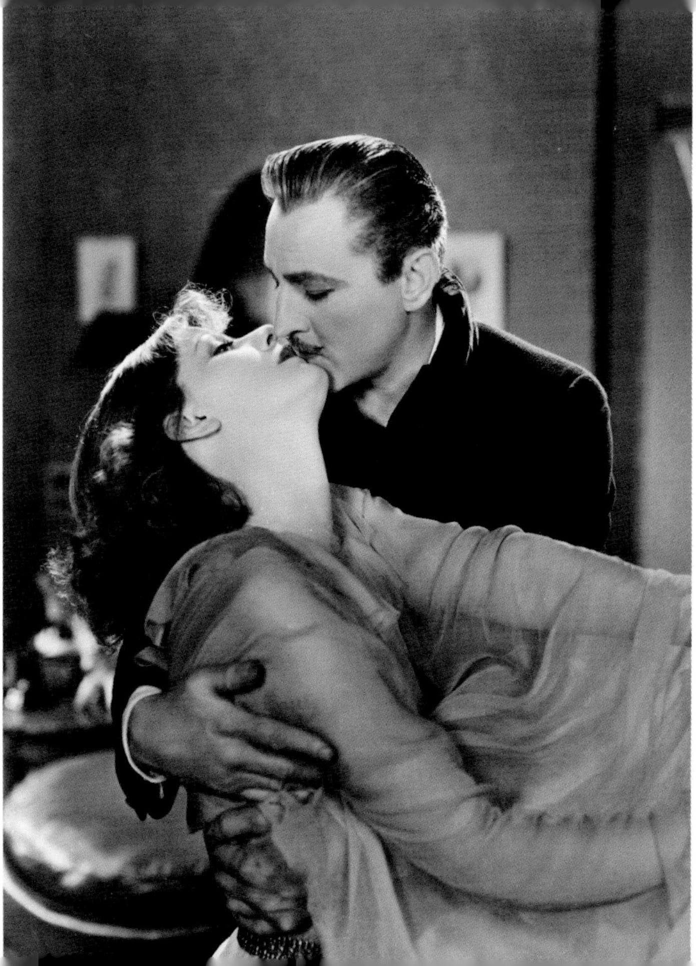

On the last analysis then, love is life.
Love never faileth, and life never
faileth so long as there is love.

Henry Drummond

♥♥ GRAND HOTEL [1932]
John Barrymore & Greta Garbo

FILM FACT: Garbo, who detested tardiness and Marlene Dietrich equally, insisted on having top billing, so in retaliation, Joan Crawford played Dietrich records constantly between shots, and went to great lengths to come onto the set late to drive Garbo mad.

Picture Credits

All images John Kobal Foundation/Hulton Archive unless otherwise specified.

cover: Barbara Stanwyck and David Niven (1910–1983) in "The Other Love" directed by Andre de Toth, 1947.

title page: Rod LaRocque and Rita La Roy in "The Delightful Rogue," circa 1925, © Hulton Archive.

page 4/5: Katharine Hepburn and Cary Grant (1904–1986) in "The Philadelphia Story," 1940, © Hulton Archive.

page 6/7: Rita Hayworth (1918–1987) and Gene Kelly (1912–1996) in "Cover Girl," directed by Charles Vidor, 1944.

page 8/9: Grace Kelly and James Stewart in Hitchcock's suspense mystery "Rear Window," 1954.

page 10/11: Johnny Weissmuller and Maureen O'Sullivan in W. S. Van Dyke's film "Tarzan The Ape Man," 1932.

page 12/13: Cary Grant (1904–1986) and Ingrid Bergman (1915–1982) in Hitchcock's spy thriller "Notorious," 1946.

page 14/15: Marlon Brando and Yvonne Doughty in "The Wild One" directed by Laszlo Benedek, 1954.

page 16/17: John Wayne (1907–1979) with Gail Russell (1924–1961) in "Angel and the Badman," 1947.

page 18/19: Robert Taylor (1911–1969) and Greta Garbo (1905–1990) in "Camille," 1937.

page 20/21: Ralph Forbes (1896–1951) and Loretta Young (1913–2000) in "Beau Ideal," 1931.

page 22/23: Ingrid Bergman (1915–1982) and Gary Cooper (1901–1961) in the screen adaptation of Hemingway's novel, "For Whom The Bell Tolls," 1943, © Hulton Archive.

page 24/25: Jennifer Jones and Louis Jourdan in "Madame Bovary," directed by Vincente Minnelli for MGM, 1949.

page 26/27: Natalie Wood (1938–1981) and Richard Beymer in "West Side Story," a film musical, 1960, © Ernst Haas/Hulton Archive.

page 28/29: Humphrey Bogart (1899–1957) and Bette Davis (1908–1989) in "Dark Victory," circa 1939, © Hulton Archive.

page 30/31: Mary Pickford (1892–1979) and Leslie Howard in "Secrets," circa 1933, Hulton Archive.

page 32/33: Vilma Banky (1902–1991) and Rudolph Valentino (1895–1926) in "Son of the Sheik," 1926, © Hulton Archive.

page 34/35: Humphrey Bogart (1899–1957) and Ingrid Bergman (1915–1982) in "Casablanca," 1942, © Hulton Archive.

page 36/37: Elizabeth Taylor and James Dean (1931–1955) in "Giant," 1956, Hulton Archive.

page 38/39: W. C. Fields (1880–1946) and Mae West (1893–1980) in "My Little Chickadee," 1939, Hulton Archive.

page 40/41: Gary Cooper and Grace Kelly in "High Noon," 1952.

page 42/43: Humphrey Bogart (1899–1957) and Lizabeth Scott in the film noir "Dead Reckoning," 1947.

page 44/45: James Stewart (1908–1997) and Marlene Dietrich (1901–1992) in "Destry Rides Again," 1939.

page 46/47: Joan Crawford (1904–1977) and Jeff Chandler (1918–1961) in "Female on the Beach," 1955.

page 48/49: John Gilbert (1899–1936) and Greta Garbo (1905–1990) in "Flesh and the Devil," 1926.

page 50/51: Barbara Stanwyck (1907–1990) and Henry Fonda (1905–1982) in the romantic comedy "The Lady Eve," 1941.

page 52/53: Cary Grant and Joan Fontaine in Suspicion, 1941.

page 54/55: Leslie Howard and Norma Shearer in George Cukor's adaptation of Shakespeare's Romeo and Juliet, 1936.

page 56/57: Rock Hudson (1925–1985) and Doris Day in "Pillow Talk," 1959, © Hulton Archive.

page 58/59: Tyrone Power (1914–1958) and Maureen O'Hara in "The Long Gray Line" 1955, © Hulton Archive.

page 60/61: Clark Gable (1901–1960), and Jean Harlow (1911–1937) in "Red Dust," 1932.

page 62/63: Marlon Brando and Eva Marie Saint in "On The Waterfront," 1954.

page 64/65: Barbara Stanwyck and David Niven (1910–1983) in "The Other Love" directed by Andre de Toth, 1947.

page 66/67: Antonio Moreno (1887–1967) and Marion Davies (1897–1961) in "Beverly of Graustark," 1926.

page 68/69: Montgomery Clift and Joanne Dru in Howard Hawks' western "Red River," 1948.

page 70/71: Humphrey Bogart (1899–1957) and Katharine Hepburn in "The African Queen," 1951, © Hulton Archive.

page 72/73: Glenn Ford and Rita Hayworth (1918–1987) in "Gilda," directed by Charles Vidor, 1946.

page 74/75: Clark Gable and Vivien Leigh in "Gone with The Wind," 1939.

page 76/77: Robert Taylor (1911–1969) playing the eponymous Ivanhoe with Elizabeth Taylor, 1952.

page 78/79: James Cagney (1899–1986) and Bette Davis (1908–1989) in "Jimmy The Gent," 1932, © Hulton Archive.

page 80/81: Rock Hudson and Jayne Wyman in "Magnificent Obsession," 1954.

page 82/83: Buster Keaton (1895–1966) and Anita Page in "Sidewalks of New York," 1931, © Hulton Archive.

page 84/85: Roland Alexandre (1927–1956) and Micheline Presle in "La Dame aux Camelias," 1953.

page 86/87: Conrad Nagel and Great Garbo in "The Mysterious Lady," 1928.

page 88/89: Sean Connery and Japanese actress Mie Hama in "You Only Live Twice," 1966, © Hulton Archive.

page 90/91: Cary Grant and Sylvia Sidney in the screen adaptation of Madame Butterfly, 1932, © Hulton Archive.

page 92/93: William Holden (1918–1981) with Audrey Hepburn (1929–1993) in "Sabrina," 1954.

page 94/95: Cary Grant and Jean Harlow in Suzy, 1936.

page 96/97: Gary Cooper (1901–1961) stars with Lauren Bacall "Bright Leaf," directed by Michael Curtiz, 1950.

page 98/99: Rita Hayworth (1918–1987) and Stewart Granger (1913–1993) in "Salome," 1953.

page 100/101: Burt Lancaster (1913–1994) and Deborah Kerr in "From Here to Eternity," 1953.

page 102/103: John Gilbert (1899–1936) and Lillian Gish (1893–1993) in the film "La Boheme," 1925.

page 104/105: Spencer Tracy and Katharine Hepburn in "Without Love," 1945, Hulton Archive.

page 106/107: Clark Gable (1901–1960) and Constance Bennett (1904–1965) in "After Office Hours," 1935.

page 108/109: John Barrymore (1882–1942) and Greta Garbo (1905–1990) in "Grand Hotel," 1932.

Copyright © 2002 MQ Publications Limited

This edition published in 2002 by MQ Publications Ltd exclusively for Hallmark Cards, Inc.

www.hallmark.com

All rights reserved. No part of this publication may be reproduced or transmitted
in any form or by any means, electronic or mechanical, including photocopy,
recording, or any information storage and retrieval system now known or to be
invented without permission in writing from the publishers.

Printed and bound in China

2 3 4 5 6 7 8 9 10

Cover design: John Casey
Design: Alexia Smith
Text research: David Baird
Picture ressearch: Suzie Green
Series Editor: Kate John